LOVE, BALANCE, THE QUEST

By

T.D. MARTIN

Copyright © 2013 T.D. Martin

ISBN -- 13: 978-1484891520

ISBN – 10: 148489152X

Chapter 1

Meetings

A fine balance exists within men, women, and their relationships… and then there are the eight imperfections.

Call him Adam not Thomas. Unlike Ishmael before him he never sailed the high seas in quest of the great white whale. His hunting ground was the hard, dry earth, his vessel the seductive powers of a deluded man.

Taneka Mayin, a mate in waiting, searched for the permanency of love, not earth's illusive treasures. These were but trifles, crumbs on an illusionary floor. Love divine, purity of thought, the wholeness of being, these were the infinite treasures worth seeking.

Stewart Demaya lived for the great white whale. It was not material wealth that stoked his fires; it was the capturing of human souls. He needed them, hunted them, and existed for them. Universal Holdings, his global real estate conglomerate, was Demaya's vessel. He, an Ahab, was the captain, the seven directors his crew. He used his subtle charisma and his chosen seven to bait and ensnare his prey.

These captive victims were the ship's passengers; passengers caught and carried on the strong currents of Demaya's delusion.

Stewart Demaya relentlessly pursued the expansion of Universal Holdings. He purchased the Arizona Cardinal's football franchise, a chain of health clubs, large international corporations, and massive tracts of real estate. His fitness clubs were eventually managed by Thomas Adam Langston. Stewart was incredibly wealthy. The fitness clubs, the professional football franchise and his overseeing corporation were simply his hobbies as was his practice of magic. Demaya followed the career of David Copperfield and other noted illusionists. However, his abilities were so great that he was really the master illusionist and all others but pale practitioners. Oddly, with all of Stewart Demaya's wealth and acquisitions, he still lacked complete freedom. He was possessed by his possessions, and clung to them as if they were his sole existence.

Richard Eagleton, and his mate Desiree Shaya, were two of Universal Holdings' seven directors. They were loyal to Stewart and followed his rules. Stewart Demaya was all about his business empire and cared not about the personal lives of his crew. Richard and Desiree had no rules of their own. Life for them was all about desires and their egoistic fulfillment. If they could but take the path of love, they could avoid a tragedy waiting to happen.

Edwina Langston, Adam's sister, taught two noon hour hatha yoga classes at Universal Fitness. Taneka Mayin was her friend and her yoga student at the club. Taneka was introduced to Adam after yoga class one day. It was the spark that began their relationship and the love that followed. Little did Adam and Taneka know then that the path to their love's fulfillment was strewn with rocks of hardship and boulders of desire. If these obstacles were to be overcome they would have to use the tools of trust and unconditional love for one another. It was only then that these soulmates could obtain the greatest of all loves, divine love, an eternal love that is never lost.

In the early afternoon, Adam Langston and his friends, Harish Pandava and Dinar Kaurava, were sitting in his office at Universal Fitness. Adam had met the two cousins in an English class at Arizona State University. The cousins had moved from India in order to further their education and to get away from their families' fighting. Dinar's grandfather apparently had cheated his brother, Harish's grandfather, out of a large estate. They had been involved in a dice game. Dinar's grandfather won by devious means and thereby gained control of the other's estate. The feud began. Later, the two cousins left India and came to America and ended up in Arizona. After graduating from the state university they started Far East Imports in Phoenix. It became rather successful. The friendship they had formed in college with Adam remained. Adam was closest to Harish. Harish was slender, muscularly firm and well-formed. He had black wavy hair. His face always beamed kindness and sincerity. Dinar was shorter than his cousin. He possessed the same black hair but sprayed and combed it straight back. He was darker featured than Harish, his body thicker. Unlike his cousin, he wore flashy clothes and loved anything that was gold. His actions were ruled mostly by his sense mind, thus he lacked his cousin's discriminating abilities. He often rattled on about his sensual desires and how he fulfilled them. Adam found this annoying.

3

"I understand you've recruited a new club member, Dinar," Adam stated. In the back of his mind he well knew the importance of increasing club memberships and the relation it had on his managerial position.

"I have. He came to my store with Stewart Demaya a while back. That's when we first met," he stated with a slight Hindi accent. "You'll recognize him when he gets here. He's a celebrity athlete."

"A celebrity athlete? That will be good business for our club."

"That's just what you need here, another macho man," Harish said amusingly and without an accent.

"As if we don't have enough already," Adam agreed and chuckled to himself.

"My friends, you'll be impressed by his presence," Dinar said confidently. "At times he can be overbearing but that's just the way he is. He's actually fun to hang out with. There he is now," Dinar said pointing out the office window. "I'll go out and show him around then bring him back here," he added and then got up and left the room.

"Who is it, Harish? Can you see him?"

"Yes, it's Richard Eagleton the former *NFL* quarterback. He was quite a player before he got injured."

"I remember that incident. His right leg was shattered in the playoffs two years ago. He was moving the *Cardinals* downfield in the *NFC* championship game when he was blind-sided by the *Giants'* linebacker. His leg was a mess after that hit. It ended his career and the *Cardinals* never recovered from it. The team lost both a quarterback and the game."

"That's part of the story. You've forgotten the real reason behind his downfall."

"You mean the media blitz concerning his affair? Wasn't there something about his teammate, an offensive lineman?"

"That's right. Eagleton was sleeping with his wife. The lineman, Jonathan Ortiz, found out about it just before that championship game. It's believed that he purposely let the *Giants'* linebacker blind-side Eagleton. And you know the rest."

"It was an end to a promising career, and he fell much like the golfer Tiger Woods. The media came out with reports of his immoral activities. Apparently he was quite the playboy. As a result he was a disgraced athlete and a man without a profession. He lost his endorsements and the respect of his fans. Yet, he came back. He apologized publicly for his actions and then began doing community work. The fans, in their fickle hero worshiping, put things behind them. As long as Eagleton has popularity he thrives. He has an enormous ego, craves attention and thrives on flattery."

"That's something I really like about you." Adam said.

"What is?"

"The way you see through things. Your views are forthright and honest."

"Why thank you, Adam. But I must remind you that I don't flatter easily."

They both laughed.

"My sister will be here soon for the noon hour yoga class. How are the two of you getting along?"

5

"Very nicely, I'm happy to say. Now I have two friends in the same family. By the way, Edwina is bringing a new friend along today. You might find her to your liking."

"What are you and Edwina up to? I just got out of a relationship."

"Kory wasn't right for you."

"What was wrong with her?"

"She was hollow. There was no substance to her."

"Maybe, but she sure was good in bed."

"That's exactly what I mean. You built your relationship entirely on sex. It was doomed from the beginning. Again, I say, it had no substance."

"And exactly what is substance?"

"You have an idea what it is."

"Love, you've mentioned it a few times."

Dinar returned; a tall, blond-haired man followed him into the office. "Adam, I have a new member for you, Richard Eagleton."

Adam stood up and shook hands with Dinar's friend.

"Welcome to the club, Richard. I'm Adam Langston. Please sit down."

Richard nodded at Harish and then sat down beside him. "I haven't seen you in a while," he told him" "What have you been doing lately?"

"I've been staying out of trouble."

"You stay out of trouble? That's a joke, you never get into trouble," Richard said winking at Dinar. "On the other hand, your cousin and I enjoy getting into trouble."

Adam interrupted them. "What may I do for you today, Richard?"

"Call me Rich."

"That's right you are rich," Dinar pointed out.

"That's what the *NFL* does for their star quarterbacks," Richard boasted. "Sign me up for a year, Adam. I'll pay for it in advance."

"While you two finish your business, Harish and I will go change. Adam will point out the locker room for you, Rich."

"All right, Dinar, I'll see you shortly," Richard told him.

Richard filled out the membership contract. After he was done Adam led him to the locker room. Then he returned to his office, entered the contract's data into his computer, separated the two page form, and filed one of them away. Richard had not taken the original page so Adam folded it and put it into his pocket. He worked a while longer and then went out to the main exercise floor. It was a large, open area surrounded by offices, studios and racquetball courts. Locker rooms were at its very end. The latest treadmills, computerized bikes and elliptical machines were located in the front of the open room. Adam's office was situated near them. From his window he was able to see both the exercise room and the main lobby.

Adam looked around for his friends. He passed by the cardio section and then the selectorized equipment in the middle of the room.

Finally, he came to the free weights. He did not see his friends anywhere so he went on into the men's locker room. Richard, clad only in gym shorts, was standing in front of the full-length mirror next to the lockers. Adam quietly watched him flexing the muscles on his symmetrical body. For some reason the ceiling lighting dimmed briefly, Richard's mirrored image became distorted, and a six inch scar on his right thigh came into view. He hit another pose and the scar vanished from the mirror. Adam coughed slightly and then approached the retired athlete.

"What do you say, not bad huh, Adam? I worked hard creating this body."

"Evidently so. What are you doing now that you're not playing football?"

"I'm playing other things."

"What do you mean?"

"I play. I like wine, woman, song and money. What else is there?"

Adam did not answer his question. "Have you seen Harish and Dinar?"

"Harish said he was going to the yoga studio to meet your sister. Dinar went to the snack bar. By the way, you have great equipment in this club."

"Thanks, Stewart Demaya will be pleased you said that."

"Stewart's a great guy. I'm sure you enjoy working for him."

"He hired me last year. He was your boss at one time wasn't he?"

"He still is."

"I thought that ended when you left the *Cardinals.*"

"It was only for a few months. After the mess I got myself into he helped with the media and everything else. Stewart found a place for me in Universal Holdings. He's my mentor. Now I'm a director and oversee one of the company's wings."

"He's done a lot for you," Adam acknowledged.

"Have you been to any of his parties?"

"No, I haven't."

"You soon will be or you wouldn't be managing his club. Those parties are a real blast. He lives in a mansion on Camelback Mountain. You've seen it; it's the large castle that sits up high and looks down on the Valley."

"The Camelback castle, I thought a wealthy dentist owned it?"

"He did originally. The dentist built it and then Stewart acquired it. Anyway, I went to a party there with my girl Desiree. He introduced us to his company's directors. Later he entertained everybody. He's a master magician you know. He can outdo anybody on stage. After his show everyone indulged themselves in a fantastic feast. Wine, women, and song weren't lacking that night."

"I didn't know that about him. He's a bit of a mystery to me. He does know how to lay on the charm. Rich, since you work for Stewart I'd better refund your money."

"No, Demaya wouldn't like that. He makes us pay our way. That's part of our working agreement. It's like a silent contract."

"As you wish. Well, I've got to go now. Welcome again to the club."

Adam left him and went up to the second floor to the group exercise studio. Harish, his sister, and another woman were standing outside the room.

"Hello, Brother," Edwina said as he approached her. She turned to the woman standing next to her. "Taneka, I'd like you to meet my brother Adam. Adam, this is my new friend Taneka."

"Hello," he said shaking her hand.

9

A peculiar tingling sensation ran through the two of them. It startled and confused them and they quickly released their hands.

Edwina began speaking to Taneka drawing her attention to her. Adam used this time to study the young woman before him. She was about four inches shorter than him and had a petite body, yet not small. Her legs, hips and buttocks were built like a ballerina's, her chest developed yet not overly so. Her face was eye-catching. She had auburn hair that was a chin-length bob and short, swept-aside bangs. Her eyes were bright-blue like a mirrored pond; beneath them was a short, curled nose highlighted by lips slender and inviting. He found her most attractive.

Taneka glanced back at Adam. He averted her eyes and looked over at Harish and his sister. She, like Adam, used this time for study. She gathered in his above average height and well-conditioned, athletic body. His face was handsome, his hair brown and curly. He had brown eyes that twinkled, were warm, and somewhat mischievous. His smile was both captivating and friendly.

Adam turned and faced Taneka. Their eyes, like magnets, pulled them together into a gentle knowing of one another and they blushed. Then, like a crushed olive, the oil of their attraction flowed over them.

He fought for words. Something deep was moving within him, something touching his soul. "I, ah, hope you enjoyed our yoga class," he said.

Taneka momentarily brushed aside the tingling she was experiencing. "Oh, well, yes, I did very much so. I'm glad your sister invited me."

"I am too," Adam revealed.

They both were feeling wholeness, as if they had been empty and now it was gone.

"Are we still on for Saturday, Harish?" Edwina asked from the background.

"Of course, we're hiking a back trail in South Mountain Park and then dining at the *Red Lobster* in Chandler. Adam, would you and Taneka like to join us?"

"I have to work part of the day, Harish. What time are you going?"

"Around two o' clock."

"Oh, I can manage that. I'll get off at one and meet you wherever you like."

"Okay, we'll take care of the details later," Harish told him.

"What about you, Taneka, will you join us?" Edwina asked.

"Yes, I'd like to go."

"Good, then that's settled. Taneka, let's you and I go shopping now. We'll talk girls' talk along the way. Call me later, Harish. I'll see you tonight, Adam."

The women left.

"Quite a girl there, Adam," Harish claimed.

"Which one?"

"You know which one."

"Come on; let's go find Dinar and Richard."

They walked down to the main lobby and found two of them seated at a table next to the snack bar.

"Hey, man, where've you two been?" Dinar asked.

"They were looking for business, monkey business," Richard exclaimed.

"Wrong, Mr. Eagleton, we've been talking to Adam's sister and her friend."

"Harish, I knew it was wine, woman and song," Richard declared.

"They look like they can use it," Dinar added.

"Wrong again, that's for you two," Harish told them.

"You win, Harish. Go get a protein shake and then join us," Richard requested. "Maybe you can put some muscle on that Indian frame of yours."

"Richard, I forgot to give you your contract." Adam pulled it out of his pocket, unfolded the paper and handed it to him.

"Thanks, I'll put it in my desk when I get home, and that looks like it'll be shortly. There's Desiree out there in the car."

Parked in the circular drive by the club's entrance was a sleek, red Ferrari convertible. Beside it stood a stunning woman who looked to be in her late twenties. She wore a short, red dress. Her legs were long, muscular and sexy. The dress was purposely cut low revealing full, well-formed breasts. She had a sensual face with green penetrating eyes, fringed with long, dark eyelashes. Her painted lips waited to be pressed upon. Black, silky hair fell over firm shoulders. She was a woman men would die for.

Now there's a babe!" Dinar exclaimed excitedly.

"Yeah, and she's all mine, Kaurava, so eat your heart out!" Richard's voice rang out. "Come on, Adam, I'll introduce you to her."

The four of them went outside to the car.

"Desiree, meet Adam Langston, he runs the gym," Richard .announced.

The alluring woman smiled at Adam. Her eyes, dangerous and magnetic, gave him a once over. "You're quite handsome."

Adam stepped back slightly from her. He regained his composure and stepped forward and offered her his hand. She accepted it.

"I promise I won't bite," she said squeezing his hand firmly.

Adam felt a slight burning sensation on his palm and pulled free from her grasp.

"Thanks for the praise, Desiree."

"You're most welcome. Tell me, Adam, what do you do with yourself?"

"What do you mean? Oh, I see. I manage Universal Fitness."

She looked at his shorts and club T shirt. "You have nice legs. What are you doing for them?"

"I work out at the club and I hike as much as possible."

"Sounds like fun, maybe we can have an outing sometime."

"That would fun for all of us," Richard cut in.

"Rich, I want to join the club. Take care of it for me, Darling."

"Your wish is my command. Adam, add Desiree to my membership. I'll pay for her on Thursday, that's when I'll be working my legs," he said and then pointed to them and flexed his quads.

"Richard, what an ego you have," Harish exclaimed.

"Rich likes to be number one," Desiree reminded him.

"That's right, Darling," Richard admitted. "I'm the man," he added half seriously.

"It's time for us to go. Richard is taking me out dancing tonight."

"And I know what that means. I'm going to have to buy you a new dress."

"But of course, Darling, you want me looking my best. Why not show off your trophy?"

"You win," Richard said climbing into the Ferrari. Desiree waved at the three men standing by the car, sat back down in the driver's seat, shifted the car into gear, and they drove off.

"Quite a pair," Adam mused out loud.

"They're a handful," Harish replied. "Come on, Dinar, it's time to for us to get back to the store."

"Have a good sales' day," Adam wished them.

The cousins left and then Adam returned to his office. He settled in at his desk, turned on the computer and printed out the reports he needed for his three-thirty appointment with Stewart Demaya. He knew Stewart would be pleased with them. The past winter's quarterly sales had exceeded last years and the club's membership was up. Stewart always wanted more members. In fact, he liked an increase in membership more that he liked the money.

Adam stapled the papers together and placed the packet into his briefcase and then phoned the front desk. He reminded the woman on the other end that Mr. Demaya would be arriving soon and that he would be in conference with him at three-thirty.

Adam still had time left before the meeting. He sat back in his chair and reflected on his interesting day. He had met two completely different women. There was something special about Edwina's friend, he thought, something about her he liked. And, obviously, whatever it was, it was still sticking in his mind, even after having met Desiree, the most sensual and sexually desirable woman he had

14

ever laid his eyes on. Funny that he hadn't thought of her first. But Taneka … just who is this Taneka Mayin anyway? He needed to ask his sister about her after work.

The phone rang next to Adam startling him. He picked up the receiver. "Hello."

"Good afternoon, Adam. I'm ready for our meeting. Please be sure to bring the reports with you."

"I'm on my way, Demaya."

Adam placed the receiver back down and grabbed his briefcase. He left the room, walked through the lobby, passed the front desk, and then climbed part way up the stairway next to it. He stopped there.

"Lisa," he called down to the woman below him, "I'm on my way to see Mr. Demaya. Hold my calls."

"Shall do. Have a good meeting."

Adam skipped up the remaining steps and then followed the front hallway, as he did so he inspected the open gym beneath him. The rush of afternoon members was still a half hour away and most of the equipment was unoccupied. Typical, he thought. As he went on the hallway began to curve. He passed a conference room and two offices then came to Stewart's room at the end of the hall. The door was open. Stewart Demaya's tall figure was standing a few feet away. His dark, handsome face topped by long, well-groomed black hair stared piercingly into Adam.

"Come in, young man." Stewart was wearing a scarlet colored sport shirt with an. embroidered logo of a globe. Underneath the globe were the words 'Universal Holdings.'

Adam entered the office.

15

"How do you like my view?" Stewart asked him.

Adam looked out the large window in front of him. The club's front entrance and its parking lot were easily visible. "It's quite impressive, Mr. Demaya."

"Now take a look the other way. What do you think?"

Adam glanced through the window next to the doorway he had just entered. The hallway's curvature made it possible to see the second floor's rooms as well as the exercise area below them.

"I see you don't miss anything, sir."

Stewart smiled. "I never do. Come, let's sit at the table."

Stewart led Adam to an elongated table that was in front of the large window. The table was solid mahogany as was the room's other furniture. First class, Adam thought.

"I have the reports you want in my briefcase, Mr. Demaya."

"Adam, you don't need to be so formal. My name's Stewart. I like to think that all of my people at Universal Holdings are one big happy family."

"Okay, Stewart," Adam said and then sat down.

"That's better," Stewart told him sitting down next to him. "How have you been? Are you enjoying your work here?"

"I'm fine. The position you've provided me fits me well."

"Of course it does. I wouldn't have given it to you if I thought otherwise. I see in you a bright future, a rising star. You know what stardom brings, don't you?" He asked then answered his own question. "It's fulfillment of your dreams. You stay with me and you will acquire everything you desire, be they cars, yachts, luxury homes or beautiful women. That and more is what I offer you. How do you feel about all of this?"

"Well, sir, Stewart, it all seems quite overwhelming."

"Adam, that's only natural. You have the world waiting at your door. Now is the time to enter that world and seize from it what you want. Don't you agree?"

"Yes, I think so."

"Good, very good. Let's see those reports now."

Adam opened his briefcase, took out the stapled papers and handed them to him.

Stewart read through them. "Very nice, you're doing a fine job. I'm most pleased to see that our club's membership has increased."

"Thank you, I knew you'd be satisfied."

"And that I am, that I am. Adam, you must remember this. It's a numbers game, just a numbers game. The more we have the more we all have. Seek out the material things, that's where you will find success and the answers to all your dreams."

"I'll do my best."

"I'm going to have a social gathering soon. It should be the right time for you. I want you to meet my corporate officers."

"The corporate officers?" Adam questioned.

"Yes, they are my most valued assistants at Universal Holdings. They are seven in number and they serve as directors on the company's board with me. When you learn their ways your future in Universal Holdings will be firmly secured."

"I'll look forward to meeting your directors. However, I believe I've already met one of them."

"And who would that be?"

"Richard Eagleton. He joined the club today. Dinar Kaurava invited him."

"I'm glad to hear that."

"I've known Dinar and his cousin Harish since college. Anyway, Richard joined the club and he told me he was one of your officers."

"He's made himself a valuable asset as has his lovely girl Desiree."

"I met her today also."

"Then you've met two of my directors. What do you think of her?"

"She's a bombshell, her name fits her well."

"Desiree has her valuable parts," Stewart answered and then his face became serious and he went silent. After a few moments he said, "Adam, I look forward to your growth within the company. When the timing is right you'll meet the rest of my crew. I'm glad we had this meeting today."

"It's been informative," Adam claimed.

"What can you tell me about her, Sis?" Adam asked Edwina. The two siblings, much alike in appearance, were standing out on Adam's balcony. Behind them, in the distance, was Camelback Mountain.

A soft breeze blew at Edwina's short brown hair. "You're quite taken by Taneka."

"It's that obvious?"

"Yes, Harish and I saw that at once. It's the reason he invited you both along Saturday."

Adam sighed. "Sis, I can hardly keep my mind off her."

"And she you also."

"What did you say?"

"You heard me. Taneka wants to know everything about you. You were all she talked about after we left you today."

"There's something about her, Edwina, something I can't put my finger on. I feel that I know her. What do you think?"

"It's not what I think, it's what you think. What does your intuition tell you?"

"My intuition? That's for you women, what do men know about intuition?"

"More than you apparently realize, Adam. Men have intuition and emotions. It's not all reasoning that's going on inside you guys. The only difference between men and women is that men are dominated by reason and women by emotion."

"I agree."

"I believe that because women don't try to analyze everything they're more open to their feelings. Thus, intuition comes more naturally for them," Edwina explained.

"Not bad, I like the way you analyzed that one."

"Very funny, Brother."

"I thought so. Tell me more about Taneka."

"She started working at the veterinary clinic about a month ago. We began having our lunches together shortly after that. She wondered why I wasn't there on Tuesdays and Thursdays and I told her about the yoga classes I teach. She said she used to practice hatha yoga and wanted to do it again. So I brought her with me to the club today. Aren't you glad I did?"

"Are you sure there isn't more to this, Sis? Did you set things up between us?"

"Let's just say I had a hunch about you two."

"Your intuition again?" Adam said chuckling to himself.

"If you want to call it that."

"Come on, you know I'm attracted to her body type."

"It's not that and you know it. Don't knock a woman's intuition, Adam."

"So you brought her to the club and introduced us and it's not by chance?"

"You know I don't believe in chance. If something happens between the two of you then it's supposed to happen and that's it."

Adam shook his head. "No chance, no luck, you and your ways, Edwina. What a sister I have."

"And what a brother I have."

Adam's mood changed and with it he became pensive.

Edwina knotted her brows. "What are you thinking about?"

"About the mountain behind you and what's on it."

"What do you mean?"

"Well, Sis, you know the castle that's up there?"

"You mean the one the dentist built? What about it?"

"That's where Stewart Demaya lives."

"Your boss?"

"Yes. He's a billionaire. Someday I might want a place like that."

"Why would you want such a large, attention getting home, Adam?"

"I don't really know, maybe it will be a way of rewarding myself."

"I see. And how are you going to go about acquiring it?"

"Hard work and keeping my eye out for opportunities, that's how. Stewart wants me to meet his officers. I think he might be planning a larger position for me in his company, Universal Holdings."

"It might be all right for you but don't go overboard in your pursuits and let your possessions possess you."

Adam fell asleep that night with the patter of rain upon the window panes and the dull growling of distant thunder. The March weather had changed suddenly and the Valley of the Sun was receiving a rare taste of spring rain.

"Hey, Adam, what's happening?"

"Oh hi, Dinar, come on in. Who's that with you?" Adam asked glancing at his desk's clock. It was eleven thirty.

An attractive, dark featured woman with long, silky black hair was standing next to Dinar.

"Adam, this is my new girl Melia Melise."

"Glad to meet you, Melia," Adam said and then went to her and they shook hands. What brings you by today?"

"I'm here to workout."

"With Dinar?"

21

"No, he'll be with Rich, I'll be with Desiree. How much is your daily rate, Adam?"

"Ten dollars but it's on me today. Take the pass I'm giving you to the front desk. Be sure to sign the guest register." Adam reached into his desk, took out a pass and handed it to her.

"Come on my macho man. We'll take care of this and then wait for our friends in the lobby," she told Dinar and then glanced back at Adam and gave him a once over. "I'm impressed with your equipment. I'll look forward to what the club has to offer."

Adam blushed. "Thanks. I'll be out shortly to show you around if you like."

"I'd like that very much."

Dinar and Melia wrapped their arms tightly around one another and left. Adam watched them make their way to the lobby. Melia's tight lavender shorts revealed small hips and well-formed buttocks. He shook his head. What, he asked himself, has Dinar got himself into now? He sure likes his women and the hotter the better.

Adam returned to his work. After twenty minutes or so he decided to take a break so he could meet up with Dinar and the others. He went out to the front lobby; the four he sought were sitting together on a bench that was there.

Desiree saw him coming. "Ah, there you are. I'm ready for you to sign me up in this wonderful club of yours."

"I'll do that and show you around, if you like."

"What do you think, Melia, will we be safe with this good looking guy."

Melia eyed him dangerously through her long eyelashes. "I don't know, Desiree, he looks hot, awfully hot."

Richard joined in the fun. "Be careful now, Adam just might set you two on fire."

"You guys are laying it on rather thick," Adam told them.

"Adam," Richard said, "Dinar and I will be in with the free weights working our legs. I'll square up with you for Desiree's membership after I've showered."

The two men left. Adam turned to the women. "Okay, let's go on that tour now. However, I think I may be the one in trouble."

The women smiled at one another and both laughed out loud. "You're safe for now," Desiree divulged.

After they were finished Adam left Desiree and Melia by the lady's locker room. He went directly from there to the second floor studio. Edwina was sitting on an oak bench next to the doorway.

"Where's Taneka, Sis?"

"She couldn't make it today."

"Oh, I was hoping to see her again."

"I know you're disappointed. Don't worry, Brother. Taneka is still planning on going Saturday. She said to say hello and to tell you she looks forward to the outing."

"I'm glad to hear that."

"I knew you would be."

"Have a good class today. Don't be too hard on your students," he told her then left and returned to his office.

Chapter 2

Outings

The March sun was comfortably warm and still showing its face when Harish pulled his white Subaru into South Mountain Preserve's parking lot.

"This is the starting point for one of the park's better trails," Harish told everyone. "It's in the back section of the mountains. For some reason it sees little use."

"You mean it's the least frequented and the most private," Edwina claimed.

"That's right; you're on the ball today."

"A ball that will soon be on a smooth trail," Adam burst out.

"If the trail's stones are round, she'll be rolling on the trail," Harish added.

"Like a rolling stone, she'll gather no moss." Adam kidded.

"Okay, you two, enough of that rolling stone stuff," Edwina ordered.

"Are they always like this?" Taneka asked her.

"It's just their spring madness," Edwina answered.

"Let's hit the road," Adam said

The four of them stepped out of the car. Harish walked to the rear, opened the hatch and then handed each of them their day packs.

"It looks like we have plenty of water," Adam estimated. "How long do you think this hike will take?"

"About three hours or so," Harish answered. "That's with a couple of breaks."

"This is our day of leisure," Edwina announced. "I'm taking my time."

"Ditto," added Taneka.

"Of course we'll take our time. That's while we're here." Harish replied.

"Okay, let's go for it," Adam stated. "You and Edwina lead the way."

"Your wish is my command."

The two couples hiked the first quarter mile of the trail with ease. That soon changed, the trail began to rise and they had to work harder to ascend it. As they trekked along they passed scattered desert bushes, cacti, and small leafed trees that were on both sides of them. They went on this way for fifty minutes or so and then Edwina stopped in the middle of the path. "That's a good place for a break," she claimed pointing at a nearby saguaro cactus. "We can sit on those smooth rocks over there."

After they were all seated, Adam opened Taneka's pack, took out a water bottle and handed it to her. "What do you think of the desert scenery?" He asked then found his own bottle and took a swig out of it.

"It's kind of barren but it does have its own beauty."

Two desert lizards skirted within three feet of Adam and Taneka. Their rotating eyes began studying the couple as if there was something they could learn from them.

Adam glanced briefly at the lizards, and then went on with the conversation. "You're right about that, Taneka. Most people find the southwest barren. They think it's dull and lifeless."

"I don't know what they mean by lifeless. Just because the vegetation and animal life are different doesn't mean the desert is dull and lifeless."

"Well said, Taneka," Harish remarked. "The desert has a variety of life. It's similar to the customs found in foreign countries."

"Life is life," Adam said pensively letting his arm fall near the lizards. The pair scampered off into the bushes.

"The world is full of variety," Taneka stated.

"It is," Adam acknowledged. "It's too bad we allow our differences to divide us."

"It's another part of life's drama," Harish asserted. "It's another shortcoming we'll have to face and overcome."

"My, aren't you the philosopher today," Edwina exclaimed.

"I am, aren't I? What do you expect from an Indian?"

"That's stereotyping," Adam expressed. "Not everyone from India is a wise sage or guru, right girls?"

Edwina and Taneka laughed out loud. "At least not this one," Edwina claimed and then put her arm affectionately around Harish.

Harish grinned. "All right, I get the message, let's move on."

They stepped back on the trail; Harish and Edwina leading the way. They went on this way for nearly an hour. The sun and their effort made them hot, sweaty, and thirsty.

"We need to find some shade," Edwina told them.

"I could use some water, also," Taneka made known.

"Up there on the left looks like a good place to take a break," Adam claimed. "There's shade along that hill and some broken boulders by it that we can sit on."

Adam and Taneka sat on the first shaded rock they came to. Harish and Edwina found another one about ten feet further away.

"Are you enjoying the outing, Taneka?" Adam asked.

"Yes, I'm glad I'm here."

"I'm glad you're here also. You're making my day."

"Making your day? What do you mean?"

"I, I mean you've made the day more enjoyable for me."

"How can that be, Adam? We've hardly spoken to one another."

"I feel as if we have. Being here with you is like a conversation."

"Go one. I bet you say that to all the girls."

"No, I've never said that to anybody. In fact, I don't know why I said that to you."

Taneka stared into Adam's brown eyes; they were full of mischief and mystery. "Who are you, Adam? I'm not able to read you."

"Why are you trying to read me?"

"Because you've filled me up with all kinds of emotion and I don't know why."

"I think I know what you mean," Adam claimed.

"I feel I know you. I know that sounds weird but it's what I feel."

Adam thought about what she said. "How do you mean you know me?"

"I don't mean I know you, I mean I know you."

"Wow, that makes a lot of sense."

"Don't tease me, Adam. See, you're making me all flustered. I don't know why I'm discussing my feelings with you now anyway."

"Taneka, I don't know why I'm doing that also," he said and then waited for her reply. There was none so he went on. "I know what you mean about knowing me. It feels like we've been together before and we belong together now. That's crazy, isn't it?"

"It's not crazy to me."

"So where do we go from here?" Adam wanted to know.

Harish yelled out before she could answer his question. "Hey, guys, are you ready to move on? The trail's end and loop back to the car isn't much further."

"All right," Adam said. He took a hold of Taneka's hand. "Are you ready to move on?"

Once again she peered intently into his eyes. This time she saw only mystery. "I am," she answered squeezing his hand.

Adam stood up pulling her with him. They resumed hiking and in a short time reached the junction. Three trails were joined together. "Which one is it, Harish?" Adam asked.

"It's the one on the right. I'll lead the rest of the way."

Taneka stepped off the trail. Nobody noticed the rattlesnake near her feet. The snake coiled up, its rattlers shaking in warning. Adam heard them, grabbed Taneka and tried pulling her out of harm's way. The snake lunged forward to strike her. Fortunately Adam's foot was in the way and the snake's fangs dug into the back of his ankle-high boots. Harish seized a stick and drove the snake away.

"Are you okay, Adam?" Taneka asked him worriedly.

"I'm all right. What about you? You look so worried?"

"I'm okay, everything happened so fast I didn't know what was going on."

"Well that was a close call. The serpent almost nailed you."

"Thank God that didn't happen."

"And let's hope it never will," Adam said.

The shade of the western hills was increasing as the sun began dipping behind them. Harish glanced down at his watch. "It's getting late," he told them. "We need to get back to the car and on to the *Red Lobster* for dinner."

The waitress finished taking their orders and then left. They were all seated in a corner booth next to a side window.

"It's been a fun day," Edwina told everyone.

"Taneka, how are you doing? Are you still worried about that snake?"

"It's nothing I want to talk about now, Adam," she answered.

"But you're okay now?"

"I'm fine. Thanks for saving me."

Adam lowered his voice. "No thanks needed, I'd save you anytime."

"And I you," she responded.

Adam cleared his throat and turned to Harish. "The girls are involved in their yoga class. Just what is yoga, Harish? Is it all postures or is there more to it?"

"What Edwina does in her class is called hatha yoga. It involves the use of different postures, postures for exercising and strengthening the body. But that's just a small part of yoga. Contrary to what people in the West think, yoga is not a religion, it's a science. The word yoga means union, the union of the soul with Spirit or God."

"So, then it's a practice of knowing God?" Taneka asked.

"Yes. When we calm the mind, stop its ceaseless chatter, and find our real nature we prepare ourselves to unite our little self with the big Self."

"That's all very interesting, Harish. It's really that simple. Is finding God that easy? We just stop the mind's thoughts and that's it?" Adam argued.

"I wish that were the case. Unfortunately it's not. The essence of yoga is meditation, right activity, and mental nonattachment. We've used our free will wrongly and have made a mess of things and now we have to work our way out of them. The yogi has to destroy the causes of bondage that keep him trapped in this world. He has his lessons to learn, and, in so doing, he can overcome his imperfections."

"You said bondage, what's that?" Taneka wanted to know.

"It's what stops and limits spiritual growth. It keeps us from knowing that we are beautiful souls made in the image of God. We're meant to be free, free from fear, free from doubt, and free from misery. Yoga teaches transmutation, changing or replacing our binding destructive bad thoughts and habits with the opposite good ones."

"Why isn't this religion since it involves seeking God?" Adam asked.

"Because religion has dogma and yoga does not. Dogma is untested beliefs and opinions. Yoga is the science of uniting the individual soul with the Universal Soul."

"You're saying religion is not beneficial," Taneka commented.

"No, that's not so, Taneka. Religion can be quite beneficial. But when one gets caught up in its dogma or limited beliefs and says his religion is best or that his religion is the only way to God then that's bad. Any path leading to God is good."

"Well said, Harish," Edwina declared. "Here's our waitress now with our meals. We'll soon be digesting both seafood and Harish's words."

"Food for thought and food for the stomach," Adam put forth. "May I say a well said to you, Sister?"

"You may."

"And may I say let's eat," Taneka requested more than asked.

It was going on nine o'clock when Harish's car pulled into the lot at Taneka's apartment complex.

"I'll walk you to your door, Taneka," Adam told her.

He helped her out of the car. She turned to go, stopped and stuck her head back in. "Thanks you two, I had a great time,' she told Harish and Edwina.

Adam and Taneka walked up the sidewalk leading to her apartment. Taneka's hand brushed against his, he took a hold of it. There was no resistance. They came to the doorway and stopped there. He bent forward and gently, ever so gently, pressed his lips against hers. They were warm, soft and full of life. He broke the kiss. She went back to him and they kissed once more. Her heart's love entered him.

"Where have you been all my life, Taneka Mayin?"

"Here, in life," she answered.

"Life? I don't know that I had a life before now."

"You're being over dramatic, Adam Langston. You say that to all the girls."

"Not so, believe me. You are everything I need."

"Need? Am I needed by you?"

"I really mean what I'm saying. Don't you know that?"

"I know it. I just like hearing it from you. I feel foolish saying this but I'm quite taken by you. So where do we go from here, Adam Langston?"

"Wherever the gods will take us," he answered and laughed.

"You have such mirth in you. I see it in your eyes and hear it in your laughter."

"You're bringing it out of me, Taneka Mayin. You're filling me with life."

"Are you drawing out my life to feed yours?"

"How can you say that? We're both feeding each other."

"Can I trust you with my heart, Adam?"

"You can trust me with your soul."

"Then I put my trust in you, Adam Langston."

33

A tear trickled down her cheek. Adam placed his finger under it and then put the finger to his lips. "This will seal what I offer you."

"And what is that?"

"To keep you safe and in my care. So where do we go from here?"

"I asked you that question already."

"I know, but I need your answer first."

"We both go home and let our emotions subside. I want one more kiss showing your sincerity then off with you," she ordered.

Their lips met. This time there was more passion.

"Good night, Adam."

"Good night. I'll call you tomorrow."

"That will be nice."

Richard and Dinar placed their bets at the racetrack's window. The man behind it gave them their tickets. They then left in search of the women.

Desiree and Melia were next to the entrance leading to the grandstand.

"I've got the winning ticket, Desiree," Richard exclaimed.

"How can you have the winning ticket? I have it." Dinar retorted.

"Not so, my friend," Richard said. "You should've picked Racer's High; she's the best horse in the entire lot."

"We'll see about that, Mr. Eagleton."

The two couples went through the gate and found four empty seats. It was late in the afternoon; the sun had already fallen behind the stands. The fourth race of the day was about to begin. The horses were in their places and the restless crowd waited expectantly for its start. Finally, the gun exploded. The fans began cheering as the horses left the starting gate. All eight of them sped past the crowd, the spectators shouted louder, each one encouraging their favorite, the race quickened, the crowd's excitement increased feverishly, and then it was over and only a few isolated cheers could be heard.

Desiree grabbed ahold of Richard and kissed him. "We've done it!" She shouted. "How much have we won?"

"A few thousand, give or take a dollar or two," Richard answered.

"That's marvelous, Darling. Will you buy me something special?"

"For you, I'd do anything."

Melia turned to Dinar. "Will you do anything for me?" She asked him.

"If I had won you could count on it, baby."

"Well there's always a next time. I'll pick out the next horse," she let him know.

"Why don't you girls go place the bets now," Richard told them.

"All right," Desiree said.

"I'll get our winnings. You take a couple of hundred and pick the next horse, Desiree. To show I'm a good sport I'm giving Melia a hundred to bet."

"Can you think of a better way to spend the day?" Desiree asked Melia on the way to the betting booth. * * *

Richard's brought his car to a halt in front of the night club. Two parking attendants opened the doors and the occupants stepped out of the silver Mercedes.

Richard handed the keys to one of the attendants. "Take good care of it for me."

"Don't you worry about that, Mr. Eagleton. She'll be ready for you when you need it. How's the leg? Any thoughts of playing ball again?"

Richard's chest expanded and his face grinned broadly. "Unfortunately my career has ended. Thanks for asking."

"How about an autograph for the kid," the attendant requested.

"You've got it," Richard said.

The man handed him a paper and pen. Richard signed the paper and then returned them to the man. Richard then followed Desiree and the others into *Planet Hollywood*.

"They still remember you," Dinar stated.

"And well they should, he was one of the best," Melia blurted out.

"He's still a great player, my player, aren't you, Darling," Desiree claimed.

"Tonight I'm whatever anybody wants me to be."

"I heard that, you beguiling devil of a man," Melia let slip.

"Let's get a table," Dinar told them.

They went on to the hostess's dais. An attractive, well-endowed woman smiled at them. "How may I help you?"

Richard answered. "We'll take that open table at the end of the room."

The hostess picked up four menus from the nearby stand. "Follow me."

She led them to the table. Dinar and Richard watched her keenly as she walked ahead of them. She was wearing a short dress. Her waist was trim, her hips tight.

"Don't let the drool run down to your shirts, boys," Melia spit out.

Desiree laughed. "Don't worry about that girl, Melia. There's a greater feast waiting for the boys later tonight."

The hostess seated them, gave each one a menu and then left.

"Great ass, don't you think, Dinar?" Richard claimed.

"Definitely and those legs holding it up weren't too bad either."

"What do you think, girls? Was she hot or was she not?"

"I'm not taking the bait, boys," Desiree answered. "And here's why. No one's hotter than Melia and I. If you want the heat, keep your eyes locked on us tonight."

"Promises, promises," Richard answered.

"I'll bring the matches," Dinar added.

Desiree's fiery green eyes burnt into Dinar's. "You'll be like logs burning in our flames' passion."

"Then I'll be as hard as the hardest wood," Richard proclaimed.

"My flames will burn you to ashes."

A waitress soon arrived to take their orders.

"What are we going to have, flaming embers?" Dinar asked and laughed out loud.

"No, just the hottest, spiciest meal on the menu," Richard responded.

"Let the good times roll," Desiree promised. "We'll start with the drinks."

After their third round of drinks and finished meals a band began playing rock. Several couples left their tables for the dance floor.

"Let's join them, Rich," Desiree requested.

"We'll come with you," Dinar said.

They all advanced to the middle of the crowded floor. Gyrating bodies encircled them and soon they were caught in the frantic rhythm; they allowed it to consume them. Each dance became more provocative, sensual and seductive with each song played by the musicians. Beads and then streams of perspiration were running down hot flesh. Welcomed desires, ready for exploration, had arisen within each of them. Thirty frenzied minutes later the two couples returned to their table.

"Whew, that was something. You guys were amazing," Melia yelled out.

They finished off the drinks in front of them. The waitress brought them their bill.

Richard opened his wallet and handed the girl three one hundred dollar bills. "Keep the change," he said.

The girl's eyes turned into saucers. "Thank you, sir," she said happily and then left.

"Take me home," Desiree commanded. "I feel like a swim."

"I want one also," Richard burst out. "Let's get the car." * * *

Richard raced the Mercedes dangerously up the wide street. The four occupants laughed raucously as he weaved his way in and out of the road's traffic, his heavy foot jarring each of them as it pushed the car's pedal menacingly down to the floor then part way back up again. Surprisingly, no police vehicles were around to catch and ticket the reckless driver.

They soon reached Richard's community. The road ahead curved and climbed slightly. Richard found his house, pushed the remote on his visor, and drove into the spacious three car garage.

"That was exhilarating," Desiree screamed out in delight. "Now it's time for a swim! Everybody follow me!"

She led them into the house. They reached the living room. Dinar accidently knocked a bowl of fruit off the coffee table. He bent down to pick it up.

"Don't bother with it," Richard told him. "Let it stay there."

They moved on through the house and out into the backyard. There was a kidney shaped pool with an eight foot waterfall at one end. Richard stepped back into the house, found two switches next to the doorway and flipped them on. The pool's waters lit up in turquoise and the waterfall began flowing stronger.

The two women and Dinar went to the pool. Dinar bent down and put his hand into the water. It was warm and tempting.

"I've put drinks out on the patio." Richard called out from behind them. "It's the best wine money can buy. Come and join me."

They went over to the table and sat down.

"Here's to us, here's to wealth and all that comes with it," Richard said raising his glass from the table.

"Here, here," Desiree added and then gulped down her drink.

"Another round," Richard exclaimed.

A blurred contentment filled each of them. Their emotions were stirring once more. Passion's surfaces and delusion's desires dangled dangerously about them. Above them, a quarter moon made a token offering of its light. Except for the luminous pool the yard was dark. In the distance scattered city lights glimmered turning the Valley into islands of isolation. Streams of car lights flowed steadily upon the main arteries within the isolated islands.

"I'm jumping in, Richard. Come, let the warm waters wash over our bodies," Desiree said beckoning him.

"As you like it, so shall it be. Dinar, you and Melia will find swimsuits in the guest house. Spend the night. Join us if you wish," Richard offered.

"It sounds like a plan, Dinar told him taking a hold of Melia's arm. "Come on my little seductress."

Desiree grabbed Richard. "Let's get in the pool now."

"I'll join you in a minute. I'm going to get my suit."

"Don't," she cried out. "We'll skinny dip."

"What about the guests?"

"Let them think what they want. What does it matter?"

Desiree went back to the pool, stepped out of her red dress, removed her bra and panties, and then slid waist high into the water. Her tanned body, smooth, tight, and ready waited for him. The captivation of her physical beauty like a magnet drew him to her. He quickly reached the pool's edge, threw off his clothing and went in next to her. He reached out to grab her. She eluded him and swam out deeper into the water. He followed her, seized her within his muscular arms and they kissed passionately.

"Take me now, Richard," Desiree commanded.

"Melia, come look at this."

Melia went over next to Dinar. Together they looked out the guest house window.

"Do you want to skinny dip, Melia?"

"Tonight I want my sex hot and alone with you."

"Then come and get me, Babe!" He shouted expectedly.

Chapter 3

Foundations

"How was your weekend, Adam?"

"It couldn't have been better. I had a great time."

Stewart's dark, magnetic eyes pored over the club's young manager sitting across from him. "I see that you've met a woman, is that not so?"

"Yes, but ... how do you know that, sir?"

"Stu or Stewart please, sir is too formal. You're on my team now. To answer your question, you have that look about you."

"The look?"

"Yes, the look of captivation. Who is the lady?"

"She's a friend of my sister. Edwina brought her to the club's yoga classes."

Stewart smiled oddly. "Yoga, that's interesting," he said remotely and then rose from his desk. He went over to the front window and looked out at the parking lot below him. A few seconds passed. He sighed, and then turned to Adam. "Adam, that party I told you about last week won't be until May. I would like you and your new friend to be my guests at the party. It will be at my Camelback mansion."

"Thank you for the invitation. I'll ask Taneka if she would like to go."

"Taneka, that's an unusual name. Where is the young lady from, Adam?"

"One of her grandparents, I believe, is from the Middle or Far East, I'm not really sure where. However, Taneka was born and raised in Florida."

"Hmm, I see. Well, I shall look forward to meeting your new lady friend," he said knowing that he wanted more from her than just a meeting.

Someone knocked on the office door. "That will be Dinar," Stewart announced. "Come on in," he called out.

Dinar stepped into the room. "Hello, Stewart, hi, Adam."

"Please sit down next to Adam," Stewart told him. "You're probably wondering why I invited you here, Dinar."

"Yes, I am."

"You told me not too long ago that your business has grown and it is in need of a capital injection," Stewart told him. Turning to Adam he asked, "Do you own your own home?"

"No, I don't have enough savings for a down payment yet."

Stewart stared at the two men sitting in front of him. His dark, mysterious eyes poured into them and made their way to their souls. He smiled his mysterious smile, satisfied with what he had seen.

"I'm offering you both the opportunity to have what you need and desire," Stewart promised the two young men. "I have knowledge, inside information if you wish, of a certain company that's about to make a big splash in the business world. Their stock, currently modestly priced, is going to sky rocket. If one acts now he'll increase his investment at least five-fold. Would you like to grab a piece of the action?"

Dinar played with his gold wrist watch. Adam calmly weighed the question.

"Well, what do you think about my offer?"

Dinar spoke out first. "Stewart, I don't know if I have enough money saved up."

"Five thousand will get you in."

"Oh, I can manage that. I'm good for ten."

"How about you, Adam?" Stewart asked him.

"Is it really going to be that profitable, Stewart?"

"Boys, it's what I told you."

"I'll try and squeeze out seven or eight," Adam added.

"Good for both of you. You won't be sorry. This deal is going to be a quick turnaround. The money you're going to make will give you a sufficient material start. You follow me and I'll lead you to the door that opens up your heart's desires. Remember and affirm this, the world is yours for the asking. Make the commitment now for what it offers you. Do this, and you'll have a bank account filled with material success. Take whatever your heart desires. It's out there waiting for you now.

Adam and Taneka's relationship grew rapidly during the remaining spring months. Days were spent in long conversations, desert hiking, movies and dining. The young couple attended two

Arizona Diamondback baseball games. They enjoyed sitting in the upper stadium's adjoining restaurant. From its left field vantage point they easily followed the game below them. Their view was bird's eye and they were the birds, two white doves, comfortably perched above a green playing field. After each game had ended the two of them went for walks along the captured river water edging the local university's campus. Then it was back to Taneka's apartment and more talk, movies and gentle embraces.

Their computers became messengers, daily emails went out, little notes expressing the joy they felt. An outing was arranged, an adventure in the towering San Francisco Mountains behind Flagstaff. Edwina and Harish got wind of it, plans changed slightly, and it was decided that the four of them would do an overnight and trek to the top of Mount Humphreys, the highest peak in Arizona. The excursion was take place a few weeks before Stewart Demaya's party.

On Friday at noon, Harish and Edwina left for Flagstaff. They traveled on *Interstate 17;* two and a half hours later Harish parked his car by Mount Humphries' trailhead. Once there the couple removed their gear from the car and hiked for nearly fifteen minutes.

Harish stopped on the trail. "That clearing over there by the trees is a good camping site," Harish said.

"It looks fine to me. Adam and Taneka should be under way by now. Will they be able to find us when they get here?" Edwina asked.

"Yes, there ought to be plenty of daylight left and we'll have a fire going. Let's set up our camp now," Harish answered. They walked over to the small meadow and set there packs down. Harish removed the tent from the bottom of his pack and spread it out on the ground. Within minutes he and Edwina had the site in order.

Adam placed the last of the equipment into the back of his Tahoe and hopped into the seat next to Taneka. "We're finally getting under way, sorry I was late, Tan."

"It was only an hour. Will that give us time to reach Harish and Edwina on the mountain before it nightfall?"

"That won't be a problem."

"Which route are you taking, Adam?"

"We'll take the loop then make our way to *I-17*. We'll be in Flagstaff in a little over two hours. From there it's about a half hour to the Mt. Humphreys' trailhead."

Adam worked his way along Tempe's busy streets. From the car's window Taneka gazed at the local university's campus which was in the background.

"You went to Arizona State didn't you, Adam?"

"Yes, that's where I met Harish and his cousin Dinar. They were in a couple of my English classes. That was over six years ago."

"Those cousins are so different," Taneka claimed. "Harish is quiet and modest. Dinar likes what glitters and whatever else goes along with it."

"You mean the gold he likes to show off?"

"Yes, he's always wearing gold. First it was a watch and a neck piece, now he's added gold earrings. Why?"

"I think it stokes his ego, Tan. What do you think of his new girlfriend?"

"Melia? She's pretty flashy herself and is quite the flatterer."

"They make a good pair, a flatterer and an egotist who thrives on flattery. Don't misunderstand me. I don't want to talk behind their backs. I've kidded them about their ways; they don't seem to mind. And, they do have their good points. It's a shame they hold onto to those negative traits."

"No one's perfect, Adam."

The traffic light ahead of them turned red, Adam applied the brakes and waited. He studied the road sign alongside the car to its right. The sign indicated the loop was only a quarter mile away. Beyond the sign children played in a park. A young boy and girl were on the playground's teeter-totter. The boy, on one end of the board, was up higher than the girl who was on its opposite end. The two of them slid up the board causing it to become closer in balance. Unexpectedly a kid jumped on the teeter-totter behind the girl. The board shot up causing the boy opposite her to nearly fly off. The other kids who were playing nearby, seven in number, howled in laughter as did the kid who had jumped on the board.

Adam gaped at this child. The youngster looked so much like Stewart Demaya he could have easily been mistaken for his son. The boy felt Adam's fixation, turned to him, and gave him a most foreboding grin. At the same time this was happening, a car horn blew behind Adam, he looked ahead, pushed down heavily on the accelerator; both he and Taneka's heads jerked sharply backwards.

"What are you doing, Adam?"

"Sorry, I didn't mean to hurt you."

"I know you didn't. I trust you, Adam. It's just, at times, you get a little careless."

48

"You've noticed that about me?"

"Sometimes our faults are worn on our sleeves. But don't worry, I have faith in you. You are my knight in shining armor."

"And my car's the white horse."

Taneka was already in love with Adam. Now, with her heart, she made a garland of that love, and, wanting him to have it, moved next to him and kissed him softly on his neck.

"What are you doing?" He asked.

Whispering, she said, "I just gave you a garland as an offering of my devotion.

"There they are!" Harish shouted out. "Welcome to our castle in the sky."

Adam and Taneka waved at their friends and then went over to them. They set their backpacks down. The two couples embraced one another.

"Have you eaten?" Edwina asked.

"Not yet," Adam replied.

"We have plenty of leftovers," Harish told them.

"Thanks. We'll join you after we get our tent in place."

"I'll warm the food up," Edwina announced.

Harish added kindling to the fire. A few seconds later flames rose from it. He placed two split logs on top of the fire. The orange and bluish glow lit up the area. It was now dusk, the forest and the sky were holding onto the sun's last golden rays.

Adam and Taneka finished setting up their tent and returned to the camp fire. Harish gave each of them a plate and spoon.

"Help yourselves," Edwina told them

Adam filled his plate and handed it to Taneka.

"Thank you. This smells so good."

Adam filled the other plate. He dug into the food with his spoon and then took a bite. "I like this food. Who made it?"

"It's Harish's special recipe," Edwina answered. "Come and sit next to us," she added.

"Mmm, Harish you have the makings of a great chef," Taneka claimed after she was situated.

"Thanks," Harish answered and then glanced at the surrounding trees. "Have you ever hiked in the high mountains, Taneka?" He asked looking back at her.

"I've done some but nothing like this one. What's its elevation?"

"Mount Humphreys is over twelve thousand feet. It's the highest point in Arizona."

"Have you climbed it, Adam?"

"I've been here but I've never been to the top, Tan. The timing was never right."

"Adam that could well be," Harish told him grinning slyly.

"What do you mean?"

"Life."

"Life? That's it? What are you driving at?" Adam wanted to know.

"Watch out, Brother, here comes a detailed explanation," Edwina revealed chuckling to herself.

"I can't help it, it's in my Indian blood," Harish claimed.

"Okay, then tell us what you mean about life," Edwina responded.

"Life has funny twists and turns and we often too easily take them for granted."

"And what am I taking for granted now?" Adam asked.

"Your presence, here right now."

"My presence?"

"Yes, the reason why you're here at this time."

"What difference does it make when I'm here?"

"Because, maybe in the past, it wasn't the right time for you to be here and now it is."

"I don't see any difference in the time sequence."

"Your life has changed since you met Taneka. Your values and outlook on life are not the same."

"So what, the mountain is still the same."

"That's right, this mountain is the same but its meaning for you is not the same. What does Mount Humphreys mean to you right now?"

"Well, it's a beautiful God created site. I enjoy sharing its beauty with Taneka."

"Have you felt this way before, Adam?"

"Not to this extent."

"So you've changed. Being here now is more significant and meaningful. Could how you feel for Taneka be the cause of this?"

"Harish, don't embarrass me. Are my feelings that obvious?"

"Yes, but so what if they are? They're just a natural part of life."

"There's that word again, Harish, life," Edwina interjected.

"Yes, life's serendipity, all those odd encounters we have believing they're just by chance. I don't mean fate. Fate implies that we can't change what happens to us. Fate implies destiny. I'll give

51

you an example of this from my own experience. One time I had a roommate and we had a misunderstanding. I became angry, grabbed him and we almost came to blows. Much later I realized the error in my actions. We should've discussed our misunderstanding. I shouldn't have grabbed him. I realized this much later and wanted to apologize to him. Unfortunately, he had moved from Arizona to California. How could I apologize, I didn't even know his address? I was wrong, knew it, yet couldn't make things right. So do you know what happened? I was on a short vacation, was driving along on a California freeway, and, lo and behold, there he was! His car had broken down and he was standing by it on the side of the road! At first I thought what a coincidence, against all odds I have found him. But I knew better than that. This scene was happening because I was being given the chance to make things right. The universe was presenting me this opportunity. My Creator cared so much about me he had given me the chance to change myself. That's why I say there's no chance, no luck. Things happen because they're supposed to happen. We're given opportunities to change and grow spiritually. This means there's no pre-set destiny; we're not pawns in the play of life. We're given many opportunities to erase our faults. Life has a deeper meaning and should not be taken for granted."

Adam gathered in Harish's words. Silently, he stood up, stretched, and placed a log on the fire. Then he grabbed a stick and stoked the embers. Flames shot out and illuminated the camp area. The forest beyond it was dark and unknown. A slight wind arose and the cooled air made the four adventurers edge closer to the fire's warmth, each one lost in their own thoughts.

Life was taking on a new meaning. Chance? Luck? Destiny? What are these really? Was Harish's reasoning right? Has one not experienced similar experiences, life's oddities, its twists and turns? Things similar to receiving a phone call from a friend just thought about or running into an old acquaintance at an unexpected location. Does this not make life more magical? Dreams are often crazy, even illogical, yet, when properly analyzed, many may have deeper meanings. Perhaps these dreams are about the dreamer's experiences. The dreams may even reveal something that needs changing or let go of, or, possibly, the dreams are just letting the dreamer know that he is doing well in his life.

"We'll take a break here at the saddle," Harish announced. They had been on the trail to the summit for nearly three hours and had just finished trekking the long series of switchbacks leading to the saddle. The saddle connects Humphreys Peak with Agassiz Peak to the south. The party had had only two minute breaks. Now a longer break with nourishment was needed. They removed their packs and sat down on two, large inviting rocks. Patches of snow, like small white islands, sparkled on the ground around them. The past winter had been mild and mostly dry.

"Where are we now, Harish?" Taneka asked.

"In elevation about twelve thousand feet, the summit is only a little over a mile away.

"Is that it over there," Taneka said pointing her finger to a mountain peak.

"No, that's one of the false summits."

"False summits? How many are there?"

"This hike is deceptive, Taneka. There're actually a few of them."

"It's not nice of this mountain to trick us like that," she said half seriously.

"Granola bars anyone?" Edwina interjected and then handed them out.

"I need this," Adam let them know. "How are you feeling, Tan?"

Taneka finished chewing the bite in her mouth, swallowed it, and then answered. "I'm tired but this bar and break are both helping me regain energy. I'm glad I took your advice, Adam. The extra cardio I did in the gym is giving me the endurance I need."

"The club's elliptical machines are good for specialized training. I like the treadmills as well. I usually set them at a twelve percent incline and walk at a quick pace for thirty minutes."

"That's all you do?" Harish asked.

"For harder treks I wear a weighted pack when I'm on the cardio machines."

"Edwina, you've been to the summit, haven't you?" Taneka asked her.

"It's my second time. Take a look at these woods and where we are going."

Everyone turned their attention to the mountain's thick forest full of aspens and assorted pines. The tree line ended just above the thick woods showing the trail to the summit would soon become a rocky ridge.

"Is everybody ready to reach our next stage?" Harish asked.

Rejuvenated after a twenty minute break, the party set off again for the summit. Another hour or so of trekking passed by, false summits, another rest period, and rocky ridges met them along the way. Finally, four hours after the morning's start, everyone stood on top of Arizona's highest peak.

"And now what do you think of the view, Taneka?"

"I feel as if I'm standing on the top of the world, Adam! I can see for miles all around. This is great, I absolutely love it!"

"Who wouldn't?"

"Is it always this windy up here?" Taneka wondered.

"I don't know. Is it Harish?" Adam asked him.

"This wind is mild. It can get much worse. It comes and goes. If you like we can go down a bit and eat our lunch in a sheltered area."

The sun, despite the cooling breeze, offered a late spring's warmth. The temperature was in the mid- fifties. After ten minutes on the summit and a few photos Harish and Edwina were ready to get out of the wind.

"Let's go down and to a sheltered area," Edwina suggested.

Adam and Taneka were not ready to leave just yet. "We'll stay up here a little longer."

Their friends left. Adam and Taneka found a place to sit next to a patch of pure white snow. The wind, in kindness, let up.

Adam placed his arm around Taneka. "I have a confession to make. I want to be alone here with you."

She put her hand on his thigh. "My heart is full of joy within this heaven around us."

"That's quite an expression. Are you a poet?" Adam kidded.

"No, just an admirer," she claimed.

55

"I think I love you, Taneka"

"Think? What do you mean think?"

Adam leaned his head on hers.

Taneka turned and faced him. "I love you, Adam," she said.

He found her lips. She kissed him back with the tenderness of her soul.

"And now what do think?" She asked him.

"I don't have to think, Tan. I know I love you, have always loved you, and will never stop loving you."

"Till death do us part?" She asked then laughed.

"There will be no parting, Tan. I'll love you throughout eternity. I'll never do anything to hurt you, nothing will separate us. We will be together forever."

Taneka grew serious. "Forever is never ending. Are you so sure of your love, Adam? If I give you all of me will you do the same for me?"

"Yes, on my word I will. You're everything to me. You're all that I've ever wanted and will ever want. Isn't this true love?"

"Is it? I don't know. My mind is spinning and my heart is throbbing, all because of you. You're giving me completeness. You make me feel alive and whole."

"Tan, there's completeness in our relationship. Whatever will be will be. What we have can't be measured. We are the sun and its radiance."

"Now who's the poet?"

Adam did not answer. Their words, the world and its sunlight were flowing through him. He tried to reason with all that was happening; he tried to see through the emotions that were being stirred up. Moments passed this way and then he broke his silence. "We both are," he said.

"What?"

"I just answered your question. We both are poets and our love is the poetry."

"That's beautiful, Adam."

"No, that's only an expression, words filled with emotion. You are what is beautiful. Everything you are is beauty to me."

"You've only said a half truth, Adam. The beauty is us together, that's beauty's wholeness. United, we are poetry of love."

He removed his glove and scooped up a handful of snow. "Let this be a symbol of our love, love that's as pure as this white snow," he said holding out his hand to hers.

She took off her glove. He placed the snow on her palm and then they joined their palms together. After a few seconds they opened their hands. The rays from the sun above them turned the snow into a handful of diamonds. They stood up from their place on top of the mountain and released the diamonds. The wind rose once again, and, as if a reminder of Mother Nature's brilliance, sprinkled them with the diamonds.

Adam peered into Taneka's sky-blue eyes. "Thanks for being here with me, my little turtle dove."

"This dove spreads forever her wings of devotion over you."

"My wings will eternally fly amongst your devotion."

"We shall fly now to Harish and Edwina. The wind's become stronger and they're waiting for us."

Adam laughed. "We better take flight then and go to them." * *

Richard and Desiree made their way through the maze of dining tables. Stewart and Ashley were waiting for them.

"Good morning. Come join us for brunch. The Camelback Resort is known for its fabulous meals," Stewart told them. "Please sit down."

"Thanks, Stewart," Richard said and then he and Desiree took their places at the table. "I didn't see you at work last week, Ashley. Where have you been?"

Ashley Karmas was a striking woman. She was in her early thirties, had shoulder length blond hair and auburn bedroom eyes. In Stewart she had a perfect companion, one that filled her earthly desires of which there were many.

"Stewart was kind enough to send me to a California beauty spa," Ashley answered him.

"So that's why you haven't been in your office," Richard responded.

"You look great," Desiree told her. "Maybe I'll join you the next time you go."

"Why? You don't need it. You look fabulous just the way you are," Stewart claimed.

"And me?' Ashley burst out.

"You're more stunning than ever. They've just enhanced your natural beauty."

Ashley's long eyelashes fluttered and she smiled to herself. "Desiree, what are you and Richard doing this afternoon?"

"We're going on a relaxing desert ride."

"Have you ever been in the desert surrounding Wickenburg?" Stewart asked.

"I've only driven through part of it on my way to Las Vegas," Richard answered.

"You'd find it interesting," Stewart claimed. "The state has had a colorful past. There were, and to some extent still are, vast mineral resources. Between 1863 and 1920 some twenty towns flourished within a twenty mile radius of Wickenburg. Some of the towns had been just a meeting place for the working mines and some of those mines lasted only a few years. Back then there had been abundant water and feed for stock as well as game to hunt. Most of the buildings around the mines consisted of wood floors with canvas sides and roofs. Few towns had stone or brick buildings. If a town dried up the residents would move to more prosperous communities. Wickenburg is an interesting place. I go there from time to time to check on the Vulture Mine."

"Why that particular mine?" Desiree wanted to know.

"Because I own it and it's still profitable."

"What don't you own, Stewart? It seems you have you hand in everything."

Stewart rolled his eyes and thrust his dark, handsome head up. "Well," he said, "That's my goal, that's what gives life meaning. There's nothing else. What the world offers we take. That's what success is, be it goldmines, land or Lamborghinis."

"You ought to know," Richard told him.

The two couples dined for an hour and then Richard and Desiree left for their outing.

"What do you think, Stewart, are they still fully under our control?" Ashley asked after they were gone.

"I don't see any problems. Rich is a good recruiter for Universal Holdings and he's still chasing women. Desiree's working hard finding new product to offer the desire seeking public. More importantly, she's completely satisfied with her part as an object of desire. Her ego loves it."

"That's good. With the two of them we have two large egos where we want them."

"We must see that things stay that way," Stewart declared revealing an evil look in his eyes. "The ego is our friend," he added. Then the two of them laughed out loud.

How much further is it?" Desiree cried out.

"The ghost town's about two or three miles away," Richard answered.

"We should've taken the SUV. This desert road is getting softer by the minute. That looks like a sand pit up ahead," she exclaimed.

"Don't get all flustered, Desiree. That's just part of a dry river bed, we'll make it through," Richard said trying to calm her.

The Mercedes reached the sandy area, the wheels spun within it. Richard gunned the engine; the car twisted right then left, and then lunched forward out of the bed and crossed the dried river's bottom. He brought the vehicle to a halt there.

"See, that wasn't too bad, Luv. We're now safe and sound on the other side."

"You still should've taken the SUV. Aren't you concerned about ruining our Mercedes?"

"It's only a car. It can easily be replaced. Besides I didn't plan on this trip, you know, we just did it on the spur of the moment."

"Well, be more careful, I don't want to be stuck in the middle of all this."

Richard put the car in gear and they drove on towards the ghost town. The road was potholed and bumpy tossing both the car and them from side to side.

"There it is, Desiree, the old mining town. It once flourished with over two thousand people. When the gold ran out they abandoned it. The saloons, houses of ill repute, and the shack-like homes emptied out. The only things left are the ghost of memories past."

"What a bleak existence it must've been," Desiree exclaimed. "A few years of gold then it's all gone."

"They didn't have a Stewart Demaya."

"What do you mean?"

"Stewart, he's the goldmine. Follow him to never ending riches."

"And never ending Mercedes," she answered laughing loudly.

"Come on, let's inspect the town. Maybe we'll find a gold nugget or two," he said opening the car door.

They walked about thirty yards and then Richard spotted something on the desert floor.

"Look at that dilapidated stone building," he cried out.

Desiree stared at the remains he had just found. "This must be what Stewart was talking about. From the looks of the area the mine must've been prosperous for some time."

"I suppose so. He said we'd find buildings here. It's interesting to see the people's choice of sites. Judging by the sunken state of this foundation I'd say those townspeople didn't do very well at picking their building sites. This ground's not solid."

"What's the name of this ghost town, Rich?"

"It was well named. This is Fool's Canyon. Let's look around some more."

"For gold?" Desiree spoke out.

"That would be nice. We might find some in the wash."

"It's hot. I need some water before I go on. I'm going back to the car."

"All right, I'll go with you."

The May sun beat down on them as they made their way to their Mercedes. Richard went to the trunk, opened it and then took two bottles from an ice chest. He handed one to Desiree. They both quickly removed their bottle's caps and gulped down the water. When they were done they tossed the bottles off into the nearby bushes.

"It's scorching out here, we should be wearing hats," Desiree snapped out. "Where's the tanning lotion?"

"Don't get all worked up. We'll be all right."

"And what about keeping my skin nice and soft?"

Richard reached back into the car's trunk. "Here," he said handing her the tanning lotion. "Your beautiful flesh shall ever remain unscathed."

Desiree poured the lotion into the palm of her hand.

"Here, let me help you with that." He took some of the lotion from her palm and spread it on her exposed shoulders and back. She rubbed what was left on her face. "Squeeze out some more and we'll cover your legs with it," he added.

The bottle slipped out of her hands and landed on the ground. Richard picked it up. It was covered with sand. When they tried spreading the lotion the sand stuck on their hands.

"This is a mess," Richard claimed. "What do you want me to do with it?"

"Throw it away. Let's get this walk over with."

They strolled together down the river bed for a hundred yards. Desiree stopped suddenly. "Hey what's this? I think I've found gold, Rich!" She yelled excitedly.

He picked up the rock by their feet and examined it closely.

"Well, what do you think, Rich? That must weigh at least a couple of pounds. We've hit the jackpot. I'm starting to like this place."

"Ha, ha, ha."

"What's so funny?"

"If this is hitting the jackpot and we were in Vegas the city would be broke."

"What do you mean?"

"This rock's nothing but fool's gold. That must be why they named this place Fool's Canyon. If the casinos cashed these in for chips they'd go bankrupt."

"Oh, and I was so hoping we had struck it rich."

"Desiree, we aren't going to do it this way. Remember, we have Stewart."

"Yes, Stewart, the magic man."

"That's right, Luv, we've placed our bets on him. Our future is secure. Haven't we already made a bundle thanks to him?"

"You're right, but I want more."

"That's because you're a woman. Women want their luxuries."

"And what's wrong with that, Mr. Big Shot, High Roller?"

"Nothing."

"That's right, nothing." Desiree stormed back.

"Let's head home," Richard snapped back.

They walked back slowly under the blazing sun. Once again they passed the old town, its broken and sunken remains stood out amongst the barren land, a ghostly reminder of desires sought and desires unfulfilled within those ruins The town's people, the prospectors, saloon owners, shopkeepers, and prostitutes long ago deserted the dried up town and moved on in search of the ever elusive fulfillment of women and gold or men and gold. In their never ending quest for more gold another town came into existence. And thus it went, the cycles repeated themselves over and over again. New gold found and new towns built; a few short years later and the gold was gone leaving the people's desires once more unfulfilled. Eventually, the men and women perished. Time moved on, a new century appeared, new men and women came into the world and new discoveries were made. The women and gold, the men and gold, took new shapes, new forms. These were material things with new labels disguising the same old desires and the never ending need for them. The old desires, desires for women and gold, or men and gold, remained within each of the earthbound people, remained to haunt them, possess them, and to forever tell them that their lasting happiness depended on the fulfillment of their desire-filled quests.

Centuries pass by, new actors enter the theater of life, new parts are played, yet, where is there change, where is their hope for change? Will the new prospectors, the new actors, dig for the same gold? Will their digging remain as shallow as the earthen mines they have created, mines that are really an outward quest for a limited earthly treasure? Or, will these actors realize that they must turn within themselves and dig there for the unlimited, never-ending gold waiting to be discovered within each and every one of them?

Once there was ant that went to a hill of sugar. One grain filled its stomach. Taking another grain in its mouth it started homeward. On its way it thought, 'next time I shall carry home the whole hill.'

The following week Adam was at his computer typing a new message for Taneka.

In the soil of my heart the seeds of love are growing cultivated by the water of your love.

Adam sent the email from the office computer and then went out to the lobby for water. When he returned there was a reply from Taneka.

My seeds have already grown and at dawn my heart flower unfolds to receive thy love. Each petal is bathed by your beauty's rays. The early breezes send the perfume of your existence to my waiting senses.

Twelve days had passed since Adam and Taneka's mountain outing. The stream of their relationship had grown into a river of love. They were like bees in search of honey. When the flowers bloom the bees come to them for honey of their own accord. Adam and Taneka's love was the flower; the honey was the sweetness of that love. They found within themselves a nectar of devotion, pure and untainted by the world around them.

The love mined from Adam and Taneka's hearts hovered above all human, mundane loves. The world was theirs to enjoy together and they began to give unselfishly of this to one another.

Taneka,

I'll pick you up tomorrow morning about eight o'clock. That will get us in the San Diego area around two in the afternoon. We'll be able to hit the beach for a couple of hours. I'm greatly looking forward to spending the next three days alone with you.

Love you,

Adam

Richard was standing by the doorway wearing a muscle top and shorts. "Are you ready for today's workout?"

Adam forwarded the email. "I am now. I'll go change and meet you in the weight room in five minutes." * * *

"How do you like our Strive equipment?" Adam asked after finishing working his upper lats.

"My leg workout was great the other day. This Lat Pulldown is pretty good also," Richard answered.

"Wait 'til you use the Low Row, six sets of these and your back will be cooked."

Adam performed two sequences of three sets on the Back Row. When he was done he set up the machine for Richard who then did the same two sequences.

"Man," Richard exclaimed, "I can't believe this back workout. I did a total of twelve sets in ten minutes and that included my rest periods."

"I know. When we first got these machines in I did the same workout as today. In just two weeks my shirts got tighter. I looked in the mirror, and sure enough, my back was bigger. I've reduced the number of sets I do now.

"Why?"

"Because now I train for maintenance and I don't want to buy a new wardrobe," Adam explained.

"I'm going for more size. I'll stick to this twelve set routine. What's next?"

"We'll use the Strive Bicep behind us then go over to the dumbbells for seated bicep curls. I think after the Strive sets you'll find three sets of dumbbell curls to be enough."

"If this Strive Bicep is as good as the back machines my arms will explode."

"Richard, you're going to be pleased. When we finish with our biceps we'll do some forearm work then head to the showers."

Twenty minutes later they completed the last set for the day and then went on to the locker room. Richard flexed his biceps at the first mirror he came to.

"What do you think of these guns?"

"Not bad, Rich. Now you can tell everyone you got them at Universal Fitness. You'll be our walking advertisement," Adam said laughingly.

"That I'll gladly be. Thanks for showing me the routine. How about having lunch with Desiree and me?"

"I think I can squeeze out about an hour."

"Good, I'll let her know."

"Have some wine, Adam."

"I've never acquired a taste for it. You and Rich go ahead, I'm perfectly content with my juice," Adam disclosed.

"Are you a health nut?" Desiree asked.

"You might say that," he announced and laughed. "Although some just might say I'm a nut and leave out the health part."

"Why?"

"Well, Desiree, maybe it's because I've been interested in health since I was sixteen. That's when I started lifting weights and began changing my diet."

"I don't see anything strange about that," Richard said.

"Maybe not today since health clubs are so popular. I once was a vegetarian. My grandfather used to call what I ate dog food." Everybody laughed. Adam glanced at his watch. "I have to leave shortly."

"That's too bad, Adam. I've been so enjoying our meal together," Desiree stated staring at him with her green, penetrating eyes.

He nodded and looked away. Those eyes were saying something to him, something he didn't want to hear. "I'm glad you enjoyed today's workout, Richard," he burst out.

"It was a good one. What are you doing this weekend?"

"Taneka and I are going over to the coast to enjoy the ocean."

"And each other," Desiree exclaimed.

Adam made no answer. He glanced back at her. Those things he did not want to hear, did not want to feel, made themselves known. Desiree's magnetism was seeping into him. She did that to men. She was like water in a flowing stream. Her flow was continuous and what she passed by she instantly replaced. Desire for her and the desire she held for itself, like the continuous stream, never ended. And this is what worried Adam. He had no need for another woman. He had Taneka now. She was everything he wanted and would ever want. Wasn't she? Why is it then that he was so attracted to Desiree's beauty? Was it her physical sexuality or was it his or theirs together?

"How are you and Taneka making out? Are your passions raging?" Desiree said, thoroughly enjoying the position she had put him in.

"Don't tease me," Adam told her hoping his firmness would make the subject off limits.

"Okay," she said backing away for the time being.

"Maybe we can all get together sometime," Richard conveyed.

"We'll be at Stewart's party next week. I'm sorry; I've got to get back to the club now." Adam rose and took out his wallet.

"Put it away, I'll get the tab today," Richard ordered.

"Next time the meal's on me, then."

"You've got it. See you next week."

"Bye, Adam," Desiree added.

Adam nodded and left.

After he was gone Richard said, "Boy, he's sensitive about his new girl."

"It's just young love, Darling," Desiree answered.

"Not like us then, is it, Luv," Richard reported.

"That's our free choice, we do what we want. And we still have each other."

"Exactly. Unlimited freedom is ours, Desiree. We know what makes up the world and we know what to take from it. That's why we're ahead of the game."

"I love it when you talk to me like that, Darling.

How unfortunate it was that the ambitious couple viewed the world through the eyes of Stewart Demaya. Their eyes of knowledge were blinding them. Unknowingly, Stewart had worked his magic on them, and they had, like so many others before them, become Demaya's marionettes, dangling and dancing from the strings of their emotional desires. Their delusive play was about to take flight and they, like vultures soaring high on the wings of delusion, were in danger of having their eyes permanently fixed on the charnel pit of greed and lust. Their experiences had become just another name for a mistake, a mistake leading ever so closer to tragedy. * * *

Adam and Taneka decided to stay in La Jolla, a pleasant beach town located just a few miles north of San Diego. They found an appealing local inn next to the ocean. After checking in they went to their room and changed into their swimsuits and then strolled out to the nearby beach.

"This is great weather," Adam claimed as he and Taneka tread along the warm sand. A comforting ocean breeze was blowing lightly over them. They found a large open area away from the other sunbathers and spread their beach towels there.

"I can smell the ocean in the air," Taneka said. "The sea and the beach are invigorating. It's so different from the desert."

"Yet the desert has its own beauty, Tan. I like the smell of it after a rain. It's like breathing in the desert's outgoing breath."

"That's a nice way of putting it, Adam."

"Do you want to go into the water now or would you rather sit and sunbath here?"

"I'm ready now if you are."

The two of them walked hand in hand through the soft sand and on into the ocean.

"It's still cold," Taneka claimed.

"It is. But how about this," Adam cried out then swept his hand into the sea and splashed her with it.

"You brat," she screeched and then reached out and pushed Adam who then fell into the sea.

He laughed out loud, grabbed Taneka and pulled her down next to him.

"You're a monster," she announced.

"Yes, I'm a beast," he said, put his lips to hers and kissed them firmly. "Come, Beauty," he said while standing up and pulling her with him. "Let's go test the deeper waters.

The next day the young lovers explored the coast.

"Where are you taking me today, Adam?"

They were in Adams' car in the inn's parking lot.

"Up north by way of the coastal highway."

"All right, what about lunch?"

"When you find something that catches your eye let me know, Honey."

"Honey! You're certainly full of sweetness today."

"Not I, you. You're the honey comb."

"And you're the bee that brings the nectar to me," she said and giggled.

Adam started the engine, set the car in car, and pulled out on to the highway. They drove a short ways. The traffic became so heavy Adam had to slow down and edge his way through it. Finally, at Del Mar, the cars thinned out, and they made good progress to Solano Beach. Halfway through the town Adam spotted a gym on his right. He found an open space in front of it, pulled in and parked there.

"Tan, if you don't mind, I'd like to check this club out. Do you want to come in with me? We won't be but a short while."

"No, I'll wait in the car for you."

Adam came back twenty minutes later. "I hope I wasn't too long."

"You weren't," Taneka told him. "Did you find anything interesting?"

"They have good equipment. I like trying new pieces out. It gives me ideas for my club. Well, shall we move along now?

After a short drive they came to Encinitas. On the ocean side of the coastal highway there was a tall, tower-like structure that was part of a long, gated area. Resting on top of the tower was a large lotus flower encased in gold. Mounted on the gate below the tower was a plaque that read Self-Realization Fellowship.

"Tan, this must be the Gardens that Harish told us about. Would you like to stop here, shop, and then check them out?"

"The shops look intriguing. I'd like to take a look."

"I'll pull into that space up ahead then."

Adam parked the car and then he and Taneka got out.

"That looks like an interesting clothing store across the street," she said.

"I'm going to that nearby bookstore while you shop," Adam told her pointing to it. "Come and get me when you're done."

"You don't like shopping with women," she claimed.

"I just don't want you feeling rushed," he said choosing his words carefully.

"I see," Taneka said with a twinkle in her eye. "Then I'll join you in a while."

Adam watched Taneka walk on to the clothing store then he went over to the bookstore and entered the building. A woman wearing a green and gold sari greeted him at the front counter.

"May I help you find something?"

Adam looked at the jewelry, CD's and crystals on display. "I see your store carries a variety of items."

She smiled. Her brown eyes expressed kindness.

"Yes, we do. Do you see anything here of interest?" She asked him then nodded at the nearby displays.

"Not at this time, I would however like to take a look at your metaphysical book section."

"Very good, follow me."

They walked past two aisles and down the next one.

"Is there anything in particular you're looking for?"

"Not really, I'm just interested in browsing at the moment," Adam answered.

"Let me know if you need any further help. I'll leave you to your browsing," she told him and left.

Adam perused the books in front of him. He found one he had read before and removed it from the shelf. It was *The Power of Now* by Eckhart Tolle. He opened it, read and scanned a few pages and then put it back. He went on down the aisle to the next section. A sign on the top shelf read *New Age.* He opened and read parts of three books and then returned them to the shelf.

"There you are. The clerk said I'd find you here." Taneka was behind him.

"Are you finished shopping already?"

"They didn't have anything I was interested in. How about you?"

"Maybe, have you read *The Power of Now*?"

"No, I've never heard of it."

"I'd like to buy it for you."

Adam led Taneka back up the aisle. He found the book, removed it from the shelf, and then he and Taneka went on up to the front counter.

"You've chosen an excellent book," the woman told them. "I found it to be of great help for me."

Adam paid the clerk. "Has this store been here very long?"

"About four years. Encinitas is a pleasant area to live and work in. Have you been here before?"

"Yes, when I was a freshman in college, I drove over here from Arizona a few times with some friends. We went to the beach that's by the lotus tower."

"Swami Beach," she made known. "It's named after Swami Yogananda the founder of Self-Realization Fellowship. He used to live here."

"I've heard a few things about him from a friend."

"He was well received when he came to this country from India in the early nineteen hundreds. You should visit the SRF Gardens. They're really beautiful and they're just up the street from the tower."

"We shall do that. Thanks for helping me," Adam said.

"You're welcome. Enjoy the town."

Adam and Taneka left the store and made their way along Encinitas' main street.

"That looks like a good place to eat over there," Taneka pointed out.

"Saint Germaine, that's an interesting name. Okay let's try it."

They crossed the road to the restaurant, entered its courtyard, and found a nearby empty table. A waiter noticed them and came over and gave them menus. He soon left and went over and waited on customers seated a few tables away from Adam and Taneka. After a short while he returned, took Adam and Taneka's orders, and then left with them.

"Tan, are you enjoying your trip?"

"Yes, very much so."

"Is it this place or is it me?"

"It's both, Adam. I'm contented with you and the area."

"I've waited all my life for this."

"So have I, Adam. In the back of my mind I've always known there was someone special that would find me."

"It's so strange. I know we've been together in the past. There's something to be said about reincarnation."

"How exactly?"

"It explains why some children are born handicapped and others are not."

"And why a person is born into a rich family and others are not," Taneka added.

"I just remembered two books I read a while back. One was *Journey of Souls* and the other was *Destiny of Souls*, both by Dr. Michael Newton. He's a clinical counselor who's also a master hypnotherapist.

"What made you think of him?"

"Because in his work he developed an age-regression technique which he used to take his clients back into their most recent past life. He also gained knowledge of the astral world, the place souls go in between their births."

"So, he was able to verify the existence of reincarnation?"

"Yes, Tan. It all makes sense. Where is there a just God if He indiscriminately chooses who's healthy or who's wealthy? The Easterners believe in the law of karma, which is what Christ taught when he said what you mete shall also be measured out to you. This explains the riddle of the inequalities. Christ taught that we should seek perfection. How can that possibly be accomplished in one lifetime? We make so many mistakes; seldom do we make the effort needed to improve ourselves."

"Adam, I didn't know you took life so seriously."

"Harish and I have talked quite a bit about spirituality."

The waiter returned with their meals. He carefully set their plates and beverages down in front of them. "May I get you anything else?"

"We're fine, thank you," Adam replied.

"I like the atmosphere here," Taneka claimed.

"I feel that also."

"The bookstore had an Eastern flavor," she stated.

"You mean New Age?"

"No, Adam, it was more than that. I noticed there were several books on spirituality. They weren't the hokey-pokey stuff you often find in modern bookstores."

"Those types of books can get rather far out. People can easily be misled by them."

"It's probably because they contain half-truths. People buy into that, especially if they believe they're part of it."

"You mean they believe they are special in some way?" He asked her.

"Yes. I once knew a woman who believed she was an incarnation of Judas."

"An incarnation of Judas!" Adam exclaimed.

"Rochelle said her guides and inner guidance told her that. She claimed her guides were the Elohim, the creator gods found in the bible. She was told she was one of them and that she had powers but had misused them in the past. To atone for the misuse she was supposed to give readings and healing energy to people as well as for the planet."

"What happened to her? Did people actually go to her?"

"They did. And the funny thing about Rochelle is that she actually did have psychic abilities. That seemed to be her downfall. She became extremely egotistical. In the end she died of cancer."

"Cancer?" He asked.

"Her guidance told her they would help cure her. So she ignored her doctor's advice and did nothing for the cancer. She ended up dying a painful death as a result."

"What a shame. Although all things are possible, it's a shame that we humans are so naïve in our beliefs."

"I guess that's what happens when our egos takeover, Adam."

"Discrimination and wisdom would save many a person from the ego's pitfalls."

"I agree. Anyway, that's what happened to Rochelle. She built her trust on the wrong footings."

Adam mulled over what Taneka just said. Casually he glanced up at the wooden placard above the restaurant's main entrance. "Tan, do you know anything about Saint Germaine?"

"No."

"He was a French monk who lived around the seventeen hundreds. He wrote about the spiritual life. His name is being used a lot these days."

"In what way, Adam?"

"Well, after meeting Harish, I began looking into metaphysics. In my research I discovered New Age material. I was surprised to find out about channeling."

"Channeling is what Rochelle did. It can get really weird."

"When I saw the sign above us it reminded me of channeling. Saint Germaine is supposedly coming through to some of those people who channel."

"What do you think about it?"

"I don't know, Tan. Channeling is certainly possible. Harish says channeling is real. However, he told me that India's saints, the holy men and women, warn about its dangers. They say that no saint or realized Master like Jesus can be channeled; it's too crude of a way to come through. They are far above that. They would simply appear in true vision or by physical means. Unless they are actually seen by the person channeling, those who come through are not saints or Masters. Thus you don't know who or what you're really getting."

"Do you believe this?"

"Put it this way. I've read about Western and Eastern mystics. They've had wonderful experiences, such as baby Jesus manifesting in their arms or visions and appearances of saints and angels. It's a strange world. People are naïve; they need to use discrimination and they need to control their egos. Everyone wants to feel they've done something great and that they're special. The ego loves this."

"I'm definitely seeing a new side of you. Do you think a lot about these things?"

"More than I'm likely to admit," he responded.

"Then I'm leaving you. Take me home at once," she demanded sternly.

"But, Tan, how, why are you acting this way?" Adam asked worriedly, his face white in terror. "I didn't mean to offend you."

Taneka remained silent for as long as she was able to and then burst out laughing. "Oh, Adam, sometimes you're too serious. Come here I'm just joking," she admitted and then leaned over and kissed him.

"Good," he cried out, "You had me there. It should've been me doing that to you. I'm the one that's the kidder."

"It was just time to put one over on you," she explained and then kissed him again.

"Thanks, I needed that one also."

"I know. So who's the one that's naïve?"

Adam laughed. "Don't think me naïve enough to believe in all that channeling."

"Should I?" Taneka asked half in seriousness.

"Should you what?"

"Find that you're naïve. Is your ego a threat to my losing you?"

"Of course not."

"Good. Then let's finish our meal then you can take me wherever you'd like."

The wherever you like was the SRF Garden overlooking the Pacific Ocean. In order to reach it they had to walk part way up a sloping street and go through a gate.

Upon entering the grounds they saw Spanish styled building on their left and, to their right, a set of stairs. The stairs led up to the garden. They took the stairs and passed through trees paralleling the steps. There was a path on their left that led to small ponds. Several large, golden fish swam in them. They stayed a short time looking at the fish and then went back to the main path and followed it to the upper gardens. After observing the area awhile they sat down on a bench overlooking the Pacific Ocean.

"There are people meditating over there," Taneka made known.

Adam followed her gaze to his right. "That's understandable. This garden and retreat were established by an Indian yogi. Maybe we can pick up some information by the main entrance when we leave."

After changing into their bathing suits Adam and Taneka took the innkeeper's advice and went to the cove in La Jolla. It was crowded when they arrived. They wanted privacy so they walked past the many sunbathers lying on the beach. Near the edge of the beach they found an area they both liked.

Adam spread out their towels and they laid on them. People were snorkeling and playing in the cove's blue waters. "It's a wonderful time for both of us, Tan. The beach, the beauty, our togetherness, this is a richness I've never felt before."

"In this lifetime, you mean," Taneka said kidding him.

"I've fallen so quickly in love with you. Actually, I've renewed my love for you. I've brought to the surface what was already there."

"You're so sweet, Adam. I could just eat you up right now. But if I did that, you wouldn't be in front of me now to gaze at and to hold and cherish."

"Now who's the honey," he said squeezing her in his arms. "Let's go in the water," he said when he was done then helped her up. When she was next to him he whispered, "Thank you for being you."

The young lovers walked to the sea and then out a ways within it. A large wave rolled into them. They tried to balance themselves but the height of the wave was too much, it swept them off their feet, suspended them in the water briefly, and then subsided. With the lull the couple's feet once again stabilized on the ocean's floor.

"That was a pretty good wave especially for a cove," Adam remarked.

"What cove?" Taneka said.

Adam looked around. They had actually gone out beyond the small inlet.

Taneka screamed. "What's that over there?"

"What thing over where?"

"That thing," she said pointing to his right.

"It looks like a jellyfish," he told her.

"No, not one of those things!" She screamed loudly and swam swiftly away.

Adam followed her all the way to the beach. "What are you doing, Taneka?" He asked her when they were both ashore.

"My family and I used to go to the Atlantic Ocean when we lived in Florida," she answered, her eyes filling with tears. "One day we were out swimming in it, that's when my mother got stung by one of those jellyfish."

"That's not good. I've heard they can be poisonous," Adam claimed.

Tears were now rolling down Taneka's cheeks. "They are. My mother died three days after she was bitten."

"I'm sorry, Tan. It must've been a terrible time for you and your family."

"It was."

"But why are you worrying so much about that jellyfish today?"

"I'm like my mother. I may have a problem with venom of any kind."

"Did a doctor tell you that?"

"Yes, he said it was a possibility."

"But you've done well here. You've never mentioned those fears."

"Oh, Adam, I feel so safe with you that I've nearly forgotten them."

"Don't worry. I'm always going to keep you safe, Tan. I'm not going to ever lose you."

Chapter 4

The Party

It was the best of times. It was the worst of times. It was a time to try one's soul. So once wrote Charles Dickens. Yet William Shakespeare wrote this world is but a stage and man is merely an actor upon it.

It was the end of May, temperatures were climbing daily, and the intensity of an early summer was beginning to engulf and imprison The Valley of the Sun.

High up on Camelback Mountain, the lights of Stewart Demaya's castle were shimmering amongst the heat rising from the valley floor. It was as if they, and the towering structure, were being fed and nourished by The Valley's energy.

Adam drove slowly up the road leading to the castle. He saw a shuttle bus in a parking area to his right. Adam pulled into the lot, parked near the bus, and then he and his three passengers stepped out of the car.

"Do you have passes?" The van's driver asked them sternly.

Adam handed the man their invitations. He looked them over and then handed them back.

"You're first timers. I'll take you to the main entrance."

After a three minute, winding, drive they reached the far end of the castle and stopped there. The driver stepped out, went to the side doors, and opened them.

"This castle is huge," Taneka said after she was out of the van.

"Why are we at the uppermost end of the building?" Harish asked the driver.

"The boss likes newcomers to enter his domain from here. Go over to the attendant by the entrance. He'll help you now."

Again their invitations were requested. The attendant glanced at them, checked the names off on his clipboard then put them into his coat pocket. When he was done he escorted the party of four into the mouth of the building. Upon entry they found themselves standing next to a room indigo in color. To their right was a closed door. The guide led them to the left and on down a spinal shaped corridor that ran along the back of the building. Along the way they passed a series of unusual chambers. Tapestries were hanging from their walls with matching furniture. Each room was of a darker color than the one preceding it. When the two couples first had entered the building they had been in the lovely room of indigo, as they moved along the rooms became a soothing blue, only to be followed by a heartwarming soft, green room. The remaining rooms, respectively, were yellow, orange and then finally red. This room was at the base of the corridor. It was the largest of the rooms and had the greatest capacity for entertaining guests, of which there were now many.

People, like a swarm of excited bees, were noisily buzzing about in the great chamber.

The guide led the two couples into the red room and then left. Stewart Demaya was standing close to the doorway.

"Ah, you've arrived," Demaya said greeting them. Alongside him was a stunning woman dressed in a revealing black and red dress. Her perfectly shaped face was crowned and surrounded by blond hair. Her gown highlighted a well-built body.

"My friends," Stewart went on, "I am so glad you've chosen to enter my domain. Permit me to introduce my longtime companion Ashley Karmas. Ashley has been a loyal accomplice for many, many years."

"Pleased to make your acquaintance," she said looking at them through amber eyes, eyes both sensuous and cunning.

"And this must be your special girl, Adam," Stewart claimed.

"Taneka, this is Stewart Demaya, my boss."

"I am so glad to meet such an enchanting lady. Who is this ravishing person with you, Harish?"

"Edwina Langston, Adam's sister and my very dear friend."

"Of course, you conduct the yoga classes at the club," Stewart stated. He moved closer and shook hands with the two women, studying them as he did so.

"Are you Stewart's associate?" Adam asked Ashley.

"I'm Stewart's vice-president and fellow board member at Universal Holdings. We work closely together."

"I don't know what I'd do without you fair lady. My world would simply cease to exist," Stewart told her.

"We exist together," she responded.

"Well everyone," Stewart said, "Enjoy the evening and we shall visit later. Ashley and I must go on and commingle with our many guests."

"Wow, what a gorgeous woman," Adam said staring at Stewart' companion as the pair walked away.

"I don't think her dress could be any tighter," Edwina burst out.

"Nor more breasts shown either," Taneka added.

"You're both just envious," Adam spoke out.

Taneka gave him the eye.

"Just kidding."

"You better be."

"Beware of the night's pitfalls lying in wait," Harish warned.

"Welcome to Stewart's shindig," a voice suddenly called out. Dinar and Melia were behind the two couples.

Greetings were made by all. After they were finished, Edwina and Taneka excused themselves and wandered off.

"Adam, I see you've met Ashley," Dinar reported. "She's quite a dish. I would mind spending lifetimes with her."

"Be careful what you wish for, Dinar, your wish just might come true," Harish claimed.

"And what's wrong with that?"

"You're be trapped on the wheel," Harish declared.

"The reincarnation wheel? Come on, man, this is life and the way it is. We've got to get the most from it. That's why I'm here tonight. I think Stewart has a new deal planned for me. If I play my cards right I'll be set up for life."

"Cards or dice? They may be stacked against you," Harish added.

"What do you mean by that?"

"Do I really have to explain myself to you? You're a grown man, keep your eyes and ears open. Don't gamble away your life by allowing your senses to steer you the wrong way."

"What are you guys doing?" Richard Eagleton asked arriving on the scene and interrupting the cousins' squabble.

"Rich," Adam said, "You've come just in the nick of time. These two were arguing over some spiritual technicality."

"Oh. I know what that's like," he disclosed.

"Where's Desiree?" Melia asked.

"She's in the center of the room talking to Stewart and Ashley."

"I'm going to join them. By the way, you guys are looking really sexy tonight," she told them as she left.

"See what you've done, cousin, you've scared my girl away," Dinar claimed.

"That's Harish's way," Richard announced and then addressed Adam. "You're going to enjoy tonight. You're going to see firsthand Stewart's magic and you're going to meet all his big wigs. We'll be dining at the same table."

"That will be an interesting entourage of personalities," Harish spoke out.

"You might say that," Richard told him.

A loud voice filled the room quieting the guests. It was Stewart Demaya's. He was standing on a platform, a circular stage fifteen feet in width. The crowd swarmed to him as if he were a comb and his aura a honeyed magnet of attraction. "Welcome again to my home, may its purpose ever be a source of life for every one of you.

It is my deepest wish that this evening brings you pleasure and an ever deeper thirst for this marvelous world."

Stewart glowed, the attention fueling his life. His tall, dark, handsome features and his magnetic persona projected mystery. He was a Prince Prospero holding at bay the Red Death, dominating his throng, his guests, his captives. He was an Atlas with the world on his shoulders.

"My friends," Stewart went on, "you've come this night for entertainment. You've come this night to learn life's true magic, to discover your true desires, and to find the means of fulfilling both them and your destiny. The night is young. Let us see how it plays out. Mingle now, know one another. Share your desires. We will dine in one hour."

Harish shook his head. Something Demaya had said bothered him. He did not join the others; instead, he went over to the room's entrance. He was about to step out but stopped abruptly. A loud, deep and peculiar sound bellowed out within the chamber. Curious as to what it was, he went to its source. A giant ebony clock stood against the wall. Its hands read eight, yet strangely the chimes had rung only once. He studied it briefly and then turned away and went back to the doorway. This time he went through it and began making his way up the corridor. He passed through each of the colored chambers ending up at what was believed to be the end of the hallway. He stood now in front of the closed door that he had first seen upon his entry into the castle. Reaching down he tried turning the doorknob. It was locked. He tried once again; an attendant appeared as if out of nowhere.

"Mr. Demaya," the attendant said frowning at him, "doesn't wish his guests alone up here."

"I was unaware of that," Harish answered.

The attendant led Harish all the way back down the corridor and into the red chamber. He closed the door behind Harish leaving Harish alone by it. Harish glanced around the great, red chamber spotted Richard and Desiree and went to them.

After Harish went off exploring, Adam sought out Taneka and Edwina. The women were standing by a long, winding staircase that led up to the castle's second floor.

"Where are the others, Adam?" Edwina wished to know.

"They're back by the refreshments. Harish wandered off to explore the castle."

"That's just like him. Harish is a man of knowledge. He pursues his interests."

"Have you found anything of interest yourselves, ladies?"

"This portrait of Stewart," Taneka said pointing to a painting on the wall near the base of the staircase.

The three of them moved closer, each staring at the painting. Stewart's dark, striking features peered back at them. In age, he appeared as he did now.

"He must've had this work done recently," Edwina conveyed.

"Is there a date on the portrait?" Adam asked.

She took a closer look. "Why, yes, but this can't be right?"

"What can't be right?" Taneka wondered.

"Why according to this date Stewart should be fifty years older than he is now. But he can't be any more than in his forties. Something's not right here."

"I agree with you, Edwina," Taneka stated.

"Then it must be a portrait of his grandfather," Adam reasoned.

"Yes, that must be it," Edwina said. "Does anybody actually know Stewart's age?"

"Not that I know of, from what I've been told he evades the subject. Anyway, what does it matter?"

Edwina shrugged her shoulders. "I need to use the little girl's room, how about you, Taneka?"

"I'll go with you," she answered

"I'll be back by the refreshments," Adam told them and then they all left for their destinations.

"Here comes Adam," Desiree reported to the others as he drew near. "Where are the two ladies, Adam?"

"They'll be here shortly. They had to powder their noses," he answered. "Harish, did you find anything of interest in your wandering?"

Harish told him about the locked room and the attendant escorting him back to the party.

"I guess Stewart doesn't like people straying around and wants to keep tabs on them."

"That's probably so. Anyway, I'm glad you're here now, Adam. Richard and I have been talking about truth and how to find it. Richard believes truth is gained by the intellect, what do you think?"

"I don't know what to say at the moment, that's a big question."

"It's not that big, Adam," Richard claimed. "It's actually quite simple. Truth is found in the mind. It's the mind, the intellect and the senses that reveal truth."

"Is that so," Harish said grinning slightly. "Then if I take you out into the desert and you see a lake in the distance that means it must be water, an actual lake. After all, you said our senses yield truth. But, what then, if we go further into that desert and we reach the location of that lake and we find nothing there but desert sand, then what?"

Richard seemed irritated. "What's your point, Harish?"

"My point is that the senses lie, that to know truth you must experience it. By going to that image in the desert one actually discovers it's nothing but a mirage. Its truth has been revealed. This discovery teaches us that the senses lie."

"Good point you've just made," Adam claimed. "How did you two get into this argument anyway?"

"We were talking about the world's scriptures," Harish answered. "Richard believes that by reading them over a few times and intellectualizing as to their meanings he will know their truths."

"What's wrong with that?" Desiree asked.

"To know truth one has to experience it," Harish said firmly. "One can read the scriptures hundreds of times, unless one experiences the truths they contain one knows nothing. One's knowledge is only intellectual and one has no idea what's true."

"I've met some people who are able to quote the bible quite freely," Desiree said.

"Those kinds of people are like parrots. They repeat words without any knowledge as to their meaning," Harish argued. "For those people intellectual study produces vanity and false convictions that they know the truth. Their knowledge is like that of a thirsty man who wanted to satisfy his thirst by consuming a surrounding lake. Unfortunately he was able to swallow only the amount of water his stomach could hold, and the lake remained."

"Harish, you're a good philosopher and you make sense. What do you think, Rich?" Adam asked him.

"I think the scriptures speak for themselves. Reading them is enough."

"And in that I totally disagree," Harish refuted. "No one authority can be taken as the perfect authority. All scriptural data has to be conceived through the senses. The real truth and divine origin of a scripture may be proved only by divine perception."

Richard shrugged his thick shoulders and turned away from Harish. He reached down to the refreshments on the table before him and picked up an almond. Not realizing it was still in its shell he bit down on it. "Ow!" He yelled out sharply and in pain.

"What's the matter, Darling?" Desiree asked alarmed.

"I've broken my damn tooth!" Richard yelled, spitting the nut, its shell and his broken tooth all out onto the table.

"You should have used this," Harish said picking up a nutcracker next to the bowl. He reached into the bowl, came out with a shelled almond, placed it within the nutcracker, and broke through the nut's hard shell. When he was done he handed the tool to Richard.

"No thanks," Richard said refusing him. "Desiree, let's go find someone else less damaging to talk to."

Stewart's voice once more boomed out throughout the enormous room. "The time has arrived dear friends for us to proceed with the exquisite dining I've had prepared for you. You will find, at each of the twelve tables around you, place settings with names in front of each. I have arranged the seating so that you will be with friends and others who will be of special interest to you. Please find your places now"

The guests scattered. Once their places were secured, waiters served expensive beverages. The opulence began. Glasses were topped off with the finest wine; these were quickly emptied and filled again by the attendants. Tasteful hors d'oeuvres, soups and salads were brought out, followed by lobster, shrimp, salmon, steak or a combination thereof. Splendor and sumptuousness were in abundance; plainness and the ordinary were non-existent. The room overflowed with laughter and loud echoing voices, nearby, musicians played their pieces adding additional gaiety to the evening.

Earlier, when they had first been seated, Richard introduced Stewart's other directors to Adam and Taneka. Sitting at the table were Desiree and Richard followed by Sam Skara, Jaya Drake, and Ray and Vicki Karnan.

Ray Karnan was no stranger to Adam. Ray was Harish's half-brother. He came to the States a few years after the two cousins moved to Arizona. Ray and Harish rarely got along, and, because of this, Adam had seen Ray infrequently and not at all since their college days.

Ray, who had an English father, was fair skinned and slightly built. He had narrow shoulders and pale blue eyes.

"I didn't know you were still in town," Adam told him.

"I left Phoenix for a short while. I came back two years ago. How about you?"

"I've never left The Valley."

"What do you do for work?"

"I'm managing Stewart Demaya's health club."

"That doesn't surprise me; you were always interested in athletics."

"Great party," Sam Skara loudly announced across from them. "Great party," he repeated. Adam, and the others, nodded their heads in agreement. Sam was a big man with a thick neck and torso. His hair was receding and he had the beginnings of a pot belly. When he spoke the veins in his neck stuck out as if his square jaws were the cause of it.

"I can't argue with that," Richard spoke out. "Stewart's gone all out tonight."

"Sam, how long have you been associated with Stewart?" Adam asked him.

"About five years," Sam answered and then turned to Jaya next to him. "Isn't that so?"

"Yes, it's been five years," she confirmed. Jaya Drake was Sam's longtime girlfriend. She had a worn look about her. Her dyed blonde hair lacked luster and the heavy makeup she wore was ineffective in covering her prematurely wrinkled face.

Sam lit a cigar. "It's been an interesting five years. Demaya has delivered on all counts. Of course, Stewart being Stewart, we've had to do our share."

"Here's to Stewart," Richard exclaimed raising his glass. Adam and Taneka timidly joined the others in the robust toast.

Adam resumed the conversation. "Sam, what did you do before you met Stewart?"

Sam let out a ring of smoke. "I was a banker here in Phoenix. My good friend Rich brought Stu to the bank and introduced us. I don't know what Stu saw in me but he took an interest. He opened an account and things grew from there."

"Sam and I played football together at Oregon," Richard announced. "He was my offensive lineman and an excellent blocker. Thanks to him he kept me out of harm's way. Our team had great seasons. We've been best friends ever since. He has the habit of keeping me going."

"That's right. If it weren't for me and Desiree he wouldn't exist," Sam claimed winking at Desiree.

"So you met Stewart through Richard. You must've done well for Mr. Demaya."

"What do you mean, Adam?"

"You've become one of his directors. That certainly proves something."

"Sam's a rising star, aren't you dear?" Jaya divulged.

"I am, I am," he said without the least bit of humility. "I'm now the head of investments," he added proudly.

"Where do you fit in the picture, Jaya?"

"I'm big in the picture, Adam. Shortly after Sam became a director I followed suit. I was a fashion designer. I had my own successful business. i met Stewart through his companion Ashley Karmas. She bought most of her wardrobe from me. Thanks to Stewart I was able to sell my company for a decent sum of money. After its sale I joined him at Universal Holdings. Now, instead of my limited clothing designing and marketing, I design, market and purchase whatever Stewart wants me to."

"It's bad enough that she heads purchasing," Sam burst out. "She takes her job home with her. You should see what she calls her closet. It takes up half of our house. She's got the best wardrobe and jewelry money can buy. I think she's stored up all her earthly treasures in our place."

"What's your take on this, Luv?" Richard spoke out loudly to Desiree.

"Girls like nice things. Jaya knows how to pick them out."

"Thanks for the compliment, Desiree."

"You're welcome."

"And what about us boys, don't we know good things when we see them?" Richard said boisterously

"Obviously, Darling, that's why you boys have such wonderful ladies," Desiree answered. Everybody laughed at her reply.

"Where do you stand?" Richard asked Vicki and Ray.

Vicki wrinkled her nose making her freckles appear larger. "What I like, I like. What Ray likes he likes. It' really his concern, it's not mine."

Ray shrugged his stooped shoulders. "Oh, is that right."

"You bet it is. You go for anything that gives you pleasure, my dear."

"That sounds interesting," Desiree commented. "And just how is Ray in the pleasure department, Vicki?"

"Not bad; I've become quite attached to him," she said tossing her red hair and brushing it aside with her hand, her hand revealing a rather large diamond wedding ring.

"You've got that right my little sex kitten," he admitted. "Vicki only does what she likes. She avoids at all costs what she dislikes."

"And what's wrong with that?"

Ray sat up straight so that everybody could clearly see him. He winked and then said, "Nothing's wrong with that as long as I get what I like."

"And what you like is pleasure," Desiree stated as a matter-of-fact.

"He proclaims it's his duty," Vicki shouted out.

"Yes, that's it, pleasure, there's never enough of it," Ray claimed.

"Isn't that the truth," Richard cut in. "I could use some action right now. I wonder what Stewart has in store for us tonight?"

"Knowing Stewart I'm sure it will be grand," Ray answered.

"Have you been out in your boat recently?" Richard asked him.

"Vicki and I go out from time to time."

"What kind of a boat do you have?" Taneka asked entering the conversation.

"It's a thirty-eight foot *Bayliner* with a cabin."

"What lake is big enough around here for that size boat?"

"You seem to know something about boating, Taneka. Do you have any experience with them?" Ray asked her.

"Actually I do. My father worked for a man in Florida who had a fifty-two foot yacht."

"I didn't know that, Tan," Adam interjected

"My father liked going out on the Atlantic and cruising over to Bermuda and the other islands."

"That sounds adventuresome," Ray asserted.

"So, where's your Atlantic, Ray," Richard remarked laughing out loud.

"It's Lake Roosevelt, or Lake Pleasant. This year we're keeping the boat at Roosevelt. It's the largest lake around here and it's close to us."

"Have you ever considered Lake Powell?" Adam wished to know.

"It's too far away. I don't have the time for that."

"Why don't all of you come out boating with us?" Vicki asked everyone.

"That sounds interesting," Adam answered.

"Good, we could go next weekend. How does that sound to everyone?"

"Count us in," Richard told her.

"We'll make the arrangements later," Vicki promised and then said, "Rich, please pass me that bottle by you."

He slid the champagne to her. She reached for it, misjudged her handling and knocked the bottle over. Its contents spilt out onto the table and floor, she reacted by pushing herself away from it making her plate go flying and spattering its food on her, her husband and the floor.

"Now see what you've done!" Ray screamed disgustedly.

Vicki didn't move. She glanced briefly at the mess she had just made and then looked away.

"Well, aren't you going to clean this up?" Ray commanded.

"Let the waiter do it," she said hotly.

"That's Vicki for you," he said loudly. "She can't deal with these things."

Vicki ignored him and called out for an attendant. He came over to her. She pointed at the table and floor and told him to take care of it.

The man left and came back with towels and a bowl. He wiped off the table and floor then gave Vicki and Ray new cloth napkins. When he was finished he left with the bowl and went on to help another table.

"See, my dear, no harm done," she said after he was gone.

Ray stared at her with his pale blue eyes and made a face. She ignored him.

"Looks like the honeymoon's over," Adam whispered to Taneka.

She nodded her head and whispered back, "A few drinks will often reveal a lot."

A half hour passed without incident and then the giant ebony clock struck out once and the room's lighting changed.

"My friends," Stewart Demaya's said, "my honored guests, it gives me great pleasure to stand amongst you, and, in so doing, to be able to offer to you the magnificent gift that I've been blessed with. As you know magic is considered to be but an illusionary trick. However, I can assure you that mine, what you see and experience tonight is real, that it contains a substance all its own."

Stewart stopped talking, smiled impishly, raised his arms, and, as if he were the cause, the room became pitch black. The audience squirmed nervously in their seats. Moments later an eerie light fell upon them, Stewart was at a different location standing now at the end of the room. Then, within that peculiar light, he suddenly disappeared before their very eyes.

"He's over there!" Someone yelled out seconds later.

A single beam of light was cast down on Stewart, now nearer the captive crowd. The room became distorted. Light and darkness formed itself into a kind of mystic twilight. Something moved behind Demaya. From the eerie light appeared Ashley Karmas. She glided to Stewart. A table unexpectedly appeared between them. Moments later a crystal ball, two feet in diameter, materialized on the table. Suddenly, Stewart disappeared once more. The crowd of a hundred gasped, held their breath, and waited. Where is Stewart they wondered? How was he able to vanish so quickly?

Seconds passed by; the crowd buzzed, then amongst the clamor came a scream. "There he is!"

"Where is he?" The crowd shouted.

Dinar stood up from the table next to Adam. "Where is he?" He yelled out repeating the crowd's words.

The spectators rose from their seats trying with strained eyes and all their senses to find the master illusionist. They were lost, bewildered. To their astonishment, Stewart Demaya was now in the crystal ball! It became smaller. He became smaller. It grew larger. He grew larger. Lightning flashed around him. The magical effects made it appear as if all the electrical, thermal, and electronic forces and all the material laws and matter of the universe were completely under Demaya's control. And as quickly as this all had begun it ended. Stewart was himself again and the ball was gone. The audience applauded wildly. He bowed before them. But Demaya was not finished. Ashley, beside him, abruptly vanished. Demaya raised his hands above his head, a violet light descended over him. He took this light, expanded it into a circle, waved his arms three times and then became motionless. A form grew within the circle; it began to solidify and then was solid. It was Ashley Karmas!

The crowd was beside itself in rapture. Stewart spoke to someone at the front table. A man came forward and with Demaya's prompting touched the woman.

"She's solid, she's real!" The man shouted out in wonderment.

"Thank you, Walter," Stewart responded. "Please stay where you are here. I want you to validate what is about to happen."

Ashley was wearing a violet gown. Demaya raised his hand over Ashley, a flash of indigo light engulfed her and when it dissolved Ashley was in an indigo dress, its shape and style different form the violet one. This system of change, a flash of light and dress transformation happened again and again. Next there was blue, then green, then yellow, then orange and finally a blood-red garment. Each outfit became shorter and more revealing. Each time the beauty, the voluptuousness, the sheer desire for Ashley Karmas increased. Each change was validated by the witness at her side. Each time the crowd of a hundred yelled louder in sheer astonishment and admiration.

The noise subsided. Stewart was not finished. A globe appeared above him. It grew in size and became eight feet in width. Then it descended and rested on Demaya's shoulders. Walter, the witness to Ashley's transformations, went to him. He touched the ball. Demaya shifted his position so that the weight of the ball was felt by the man.

"It's heavy!" the man shouted. His knees began to buckle.

Demaya again took on the full weight of the globe. He knelt down on one knee. The globe remained solidly on his shoulders. He held his stance for a few seconds more and then placed the globe down by his side where it quickly disappeared.

"My people, now that I have captured you," Stewart Demaya bellowed out, "we shall take a break. Please, however, continue indulging in tonight's offerings."

Stewart, arm and arm with the crimson clad Ashley, stepped off the stage and went out amongst the guests.

"That was unbelievable," Adam declared to those around him.

"That was Stewart Demaya at his best," Desiree claimed and then proceeded talking about his other abilities.

"I don't know about the rest of you guys," Richard said loudly, "but that Ashley really had me going. Man, what a dish!" Richard exclaimed.

The women at the table leered at Richard, let their gaze dwindle and then turned their eyes up the room to the reddish clad Ashley Karmas. Their look turned to envy, as if what they had just beheld represented the substance of womanhood and what they each should be.

"You know," Richard went on, "desire for Ashley reminds me of a joke I once heard. Four men were sitting in a restaurant waiting to order their dessert. The waitress, wearing a miniskirt, came by to fill their orders. She asked them what they wanted. Three of the men said a piece of raisin pie. She stepped up on a chair and from a shelf above her took down the requested pie. When she was done she asked the fourth man if his is raisin to. He said no but it sure is quivering a lot."

Everybody burst into laughter.

Sam Skara snapped out, "That would be us. That would indeed be us. And what about you girls, see anything tempting in that performance we just witnessed?"

Jaya answered for the others. "Stewart was amazing. He's so sexy and commanding. Who wouldn't follow him anywhere?"

"That's why we love him so," Desiree responded. "Taneka, how do you feel about all of this?"

"I don't know. I'm still in wonderment. Everything is strange tonight. It's all so new to me."

"It won't be long and you'll be aboard with the rest of us," Jaya disclosed.

"Speaking of being aboard, don't forget about our boating plans for next weekend," Ray pleaded to everyone. "Right, Honey?" He asked his wife.

"Absolutely, I think it's a marvelous idea," Vicki answered.

"I'm counting on it," Richard answered.

"What about the rest of you?" Ray asked. Everyone gave their approval.

"That's great. We'll work out the details later."

Stewart and Ashley walked over to their table. "Well, I see everyone is enjoying themselves," Stewart said. "Adam, I hope you and Taneka are becoming well acquainted with my crew."

"We are," Adam said.

"That's well and good," Stewart responded and then began a conversation with Sam Skara. Adam paid no attention to what was being said. His eyes were on Ashley Karmas who was talking to Richard. Adam observed her hand and body movement. Her dress seemed to change from scarlet to black and back to scarlet again with each of her gesticulations. She placed her hands on Richard's shoulders. Desiree was intently scrutinizing her mate's reactions to Ashley's words and provocative movements. She seemed anxious and perturbed by what she witnessed. Ashley was absolutely stunning. Desiree glanced over at Adam. Her green penetrating eyes smiled dangerously into his and he turned away.

Stewart began speaking louder. All eyes went to him. "I'm extremely pleased to have captivated you with my magic. May it ever serve to fulfill and hold you in this marvelous world we all exist within."

"Your illusions were perfect," Jaya claimed. "You're better than all the other illusionists combined. We are so fortunate to have found you."

"The magic was nothing," Demaya said as if making what he had done seem as insubstantial as a mirage in the desert.

Without notice, the chamber dimmed and the room's appearance once more was altered. A single ray of light played on Demaya's dark, black hair and another ray splashed across his handsome face. He straightened up; his face was full of command. The room's quests quieted. He pored over them through those black, mysterious eyes. The large ebony clock once more rang out throughout the chamber, again with one solitary boom as if time were stilled and left to be measured only by its captive resonance. Demaya was spinning his delusive powers upon them, like a spider spins his web.

Music began playing, guests rose from their seats and they, spellbound, sauntered their way to the middle of the chamber. Attendants pushed the empty tables aside. Dancing began. Fifty couples were caught within the musicians' pulsating music spinning out throughout the great room. The tempo increased. Classical pieces were replaced with the beat of the Latino. Then there was singing and the heavy beat of modern rock. The heart of life was beating feverishly; the great chamber was becoming that heart.

"This is too much," Harish announced to Adam and Taneka next to him. "Edwina and I are going outside for a break. Please join us."

"All right, Harish," Taneka answered. "Come on, Adam, we both could stand a breath of fresh air."

"But, Tan, we might miss something here."

"Brother, listen to them," Edwina pleaded. "We need to take a break."

"I'll follow you then," Adam said reluctantly.

They made their way through the writhing bodies to a doorway leading directly outside the building.

"I'll join you in a minute," Harish said and left them there.

He marched back through the crowd and found Dinar and Melia. "I've been looking for you two."

"Harish, why aren't you dancing with the rest us?" Dinar wanted to know.

"Come with me, you should take a break from this."

"Ah, come on, Harish, Dinar and I are having a great time. You don't want to spoil it for us, do you?" Melia spoke out.

"Melia," Harish began, "You both are falling under Demaya's spell. It may go too far and you'll end up regretting it. Something's going on here that's just not right. I don't like it."

"Cousin, you're over reacting to the excitement."

"That's right, Dinar, Harish is being overprotective. You have good judgment. You always know what you're doing."

107

"Stop that, Melia."

"Stop what? Dinar always does the right thing."

"Stop that flattery. It's like poisoned honey. Flattery insulates us from reality. It makes us excuse our faults and hide from them. Why do you always find it necessary to resort to flattery?"

"I don't want to hear any more of this," Melia yelled back at him. "Come on, Dinar; take me to the heart of this room."

"She's right, Cousin. We're going into the center of the action. And that's the reality of the situation. This is life."

They turned and walked away from Harish. He sighed and then hurried to the exit and went out into the open night. Under the full moon's brightness he saw his friends sitting on a bench across the way. He took in a few breaths of fresh air and then went to them.

"Ah, this is the true freedom of the world," Harish told them looking up at the moon and breathing in the air around him. "To live naturally within nature, to be free of the world's chains and the harnesses we put upon ourselves is what really matters."

"What didn't you like about the dancing, Harish?' Taneka asked him.

"It felt unnatural and uncontrolled. There's something about Demaya's evening that's just not right."

"It's only a party, Harish," Adam responded.

"I don't think so," Harish replied.

"I think you're being overly skeptical and too discriminative, Harish," Adam claimed.

"Maybe," he said. "Edwina, let's take a walk down the road."

They left. Adam took hold of Taneka's hand. "Harish seems a little squeamish at times, doesn't he?"

"He's concerned about everybody's welfare, that's all."

Across the way Stewart stepped out of the castle door. He signaled to Adam and Taneka and then strolled over to them.

"I see you've left my party," he said staring hard at them.

"Harish felt we needed a break," Adam told him.

"I see," Stewart answered. "Where is he now?"

"He went with my sister for a walk down the road."

"Good, let me show you my garden."

Demaya led them to a wooden bench in the center of the garden. Adam and Taneka sat down amongst flowered bushes, shrubs, and fruit trees. Demaya stood behind them.

"I want you two to fully enjoy what I have to offer," he told them firmly.

"We shall. When did you create this garden, Stewart?" Adam responded.

There was no answer. Adam and Taneka turned around to face Demaya – he was gone!

"That's strange, were did he go so fast?" Taneka said.

Adam shrugged his shoulders and then wrapped his arm around Taneka and pulled her to him. She placed her head on his shoulder. Above them, two owls in the nearby tree sat on a limb eying them. On the ground next to the bench something moved. A snake, six feet in length, slithered along the ground. It reached the owls' tree, moved around it and then began to climb it. One of the owls screeched and flew away. The other owl kept its position watching the snake carefully. In the background the sounds of frantic music stirred over the garden.

"You know I want you more than anything, Tan." Adam let her know.

"How do you want me?" She asked him.

The warmth of her breath excited him. His heart pounded. He put his lips to hers. She yielded to her passion. They kissed, parted, and kissed again, this time longer. Adam's hand went to the top of her dress and then down into it. He found her breast and caressed it. She groaned. Adam, became bolder, freed his hand from her breast and then put it under her dress's bottom.

"Stop, Adam!" Taneka burst out.

"Stop?" Adam repeated. His hand went towards her groin.

"I said stop it!" This time her voice was full of anger. "Stop what you're doing. It isn't right. This isn't the time or place. Don't weaken our relationship this way."

"But, Tan, I want you; I've always wanted you, all of you. I love you."

"This is not all of me, Adam. Love is not lust. I love you too. But our love must be pure and not driven by uncontrolled desires."

Adam sat back against the bench, his hands by his side. "You're right. I know it. It's just this night. My emotions have gotten out of control. I apologize for my abruptness."

She took his hand in hers, and focused her eyes on his. "Oh, Adam, I do so care so much for you, but we must keep our passions under control."

A few seconds passed then she laughed lightly.

"What's so funny, Tan?"

"Don't you think that it's funny me advising you about emotions when it's women who are so emotional. You should be the one doing the reasoning now."

"I understand," Adam acknowledged. "It's the male-female, yin-yang thing. Yet this time you're the yang and I'm the yin," he added chuckling to himself. "I guess that's the way it is. It's either reason or emotion controlling us."

"Finding the balance is difficult, Adam. Here we are under a full moon struggling with our emotions. Inside that building a hundred people are doing the same."

A cool breeze, the night's first, covered and caressed Adam and Taneka. The two owls were back together on the limb of the tree. The serpent was nowhere to be seen.

The young couple glanced over at Demaya's castle. Stewart was standing by it talking to Ashley. She nodded her head from time to time and then looked across the road at them.

"There you two are!" Harish yelled out. He was walking up to the road to them. "Edwina thought we'd find you here."

"And why is that?" Adam asked him.

"Because it's only fitting that Demaya would have a garden. It's another one of his extended enticements."

"It has added to the mystery of this evening," Taneka stated.

"I hope those caught in the frenzy of Demaya's party will come to their senses and leave his castle before they abandon themselves to the evening," Edwina wished out loud.

"Yes, we all hope that," Harish added.

"Well at least we are out of that place. Let's go home," Edwina told them.

"All right," Adam answered. "Tan and I have had enough for the night."

"Adam!" Stewart called out making his way to him from across the way. Ashley was with him.

"What does he want," Taneka asked.

"I don't know but whatever it is I don't trust him," Harish answered.

Stewart and Ashley were now near them.

"We're leaving your party," Harish spoke out.

"But it's barely underway my friend. Come back in all of you, there's yet much to see and do," Demaya claimed.

"Yes, do come back in," Ashley pleaded.

"We've had enough," Edwina spoke out.

Demaya's eyes turned cold, black, and like steel. He fixed them on her. "You don't know what enough is," he claimed sharply.

"Ah, but we do," Harish spoke out with conviction.

"You must come back," Demaya said raising his voice in irritation.

"We are not going to do that. I don't like what you are doing here," Harish replied. "Come, let's go," he said to his friends.

"You and your yoga, Harish, you don't know anything!'

"I know malevolence when I see it," Harish shouted back.

"The only malevolence is in your mind," Demaya reasoned for him.

"I'm not open to a debate. Whatever your hidden agenda is we're not falling for it," Harish said and then turned to his friends. "We'll walk down to the car now."

The two couples left. Stewart and Ashley watched them descend the mountain road.

"What are going to do, Stewart?" Ashley asked him.

"We have Desiree and the rest of the crew to use their talents on our guests."

"What about those four that just left?"

"Adam has potential, we mustn't lose him. As to those others Harish is a problem. His resistance has grown stronger and now he's capable of pulling others the wrong way."

"What will you do?"

"Don't worry, there's more than one way to skin a cat, my dear."

"It's so strange," Taneka said when the four of them reached the car.

"What is?" Adam asked opening the car door for her.

"We've left Stewart Demaya's castle. In spite of being free of that building, I still feel I'm under its influence."

Chapter 5

Observations

The next day Adam and Harish left late in the morning for the freedom of the desert. They drove east of the city in Harish's car. After fifty minutes of travel they turned off the main highway, drove on an unimproved road for another fifteen minutes and then came to a trailhead.

Harish turned into the parking area by the trail. "Adam have you ever been here?"

"Not on this trail but I've hiked in the Superstitions."

"For such a quick getaway this one is a good one."

"Let's grab our gear and get underway then."

They trekked along for an hour. Large boulders, dry river beds, hills, a variety of desert vegetation, and distant mountains decorated the trail along the way.

"We can stop and have our lunch here," Harish said.

They were in a dry riverbed. Boulders, piled upon one other, were off to their left. An isolated flat rock near them caught their eye and they went and sat there.

"It's good getting out in the desert again," Adam stated.

"The serenity does us well,' Harish responded. "After last night I think we'll appreciate nature more."

"There's a silence here," Adam claimed.

"That's one of nature's beauties. Too many people take Mother Nature for granted. She's all around us but we don't get to know her. Instead, we seek worldly things which leave us restless."

"Surely you don't expect men to live like monks."

"No, of course not. The problem is that we're never fully satisfied with what we have. After a time we grow weary of our possessions, and begin again looking for new ones. Thus our desires are never quenched."

"What's wrong with having things now?"

"Adam, we have two lives. Our outer life, which is our body and ego, is given too much importance. And our inner life, which is our soul, is given too little. The outer life of man ought to be lived in concordance with his inner existence. There should be a perfect balance. If we give more importance to the body and neglect the soul we become worried and anxious, and fervently cling to false securities. A saint once said 'know the difference between the container and the content and true knowledge will dawn within you, dispelling all fear and darkness.' The secret lies in knowing that the body is the container and that the content is the soul. Milk is different form the vessel in which it is contained. The vessel is not the milk and the milk is not the vessel. We don't understand that the existence of the body depends on the soul."

"Is this why you left Demaya's party last night, Harish?"

"Yes. He was preying on our desires. He was more than an illusionist he was the illusion itself. I was uncomfortable for you and Taneka, especially your meeting Stewart's directors."

"I thought you didn't know them."

"I've never been to one of Stewart's parties but I have met all seven directors."

"They seem to be okay. Some are, perhaps, a little edgy."

"Yes, Adam, they do have their faults."

"That Ashley is something else."

"Be careful of her as well as Desiree, they both have eyes for men."

"I can see why men would go after them."

"I think Stewart uses those two women to draw others into his ways. He already has material wealth. I think ensnaring others into his lifestyle is a game for him."

"Why are you so skeptical about Demaya?"

"Adam, have you heard of the eight imperfections?"

"No, what are they."

"They are the eight obstacles that keep man from perfection and keep him bound to this world."

"You mean like the seven deadly sins?"

"Not quite. The seven deadly sins are but off-chutes from the eight imperfections. The eight flaws I'm talking about are ignorance, ego, attachment, repulsion, body attachment, karma, habit and latent desire. I see them clearly in Demaya and his seven directors."

117

"What is it that you see?"

"I see how these eight imperfections have bound them to this material world. I see how they make man look outside himself as if this is the only world that matters. We, mankind, don't see our inner world; we don't see our perfect soul. To be made in the image of God doesn't mean that it's this imperfect body. Demaya, for whatever his twisted reason, apparently wants us to believe it is."

"What do you think it means to be made in the image of God?"

"In order to find that answer we have to look at man's imperfections. The first one, ignorance, is the belief that this finite world and this body are real instead of the eternally pure soul.

"We see ourselves through our ego, which is another imperfection. Ego is the pseudo soul. Ego is when the soul, or seer, the image of God in man, forgets its true divine Self and becomes identified with the body and mind. Christ told us we are all sons of God and know not, and that the kingdom of God is found within us."

"How do you know Christ's words? You're a Hindu and a yogi."

"I believe in all true religions. Yes, I am a yogi. Do you remember what I told you yoga is, Adam? Yoga is the union of our individual consciousness, the soul, with the universal consciousness, Spirit or God. Through man's ignorance, yoga is thought to be something that's weird and to be avoided. Yoga is simply man's search for and uniting with the Divine. The Christian, Hindu, Buddhist, or Islamic, all are yogis when they seek union with God. Yoga is of itself not a religion."

"But how can a Christian believe in this? Why should they even consider words from another scripture?"

"All religion has its dogma, Adam. Truth should be the only religion. Religionists who cling to dogma will often parrot what they don't really understand or haven't realized. When you ask them questions, they quote scriptures like a spiritual recording. It's useless to reason with them because they're so sure they know it all. Many teachers will tell you what to believe. Then they take away your reason and tell to you to follow only their logic. We mustn't allow the blind to lead the blind. Only a man who has direct experience of God knows truth."

"Do you believe there's one religion that's best for all?"

"What difference does it make what religion one practices as long as one bows to God with all his heart? All true religions will take one to the Ultimate Goal. One needs to find what's best for him, and study the religion's tenets with the eyes of reason and wisdom. We mustn't be controlled by our emotions. There needs to be a balance between the heart and the mind."

"There's certainly a large gulf between Eastern and Western practices," Adam claimed.

"What's that?"

"The first is reincarnation and the second hell and damnation."

"Reincarnation is mentioned in the bible. Look in the bible passages Matthew 17:12-13 and 11:13-14 as well as Revelation 3:12. Reincarnation was a common belief of the Essenes during Christ's time. It was abolished by Christian church fathers at the Second Council of Constantinople around 553 AD.

"As to hell and damnation, how could a God of love, the Creator of all love, be so inhumane? He's not a tyrant. Would you condemn your son eternally to a fiery hell, Adam? What father would do that to his children? And why would God punish his children eternally for a finite act? Jesus' message was about love and forgiveness. When you think of reincarnation, if man repeatedly has to come back to the physical world to perfect himself and to burn off his evil karma, isn't that like hell? Just think of it, we come back lifetime after lifetime into this imperfect world, what a hellish thought that is. You know heaven is out there waiting for you but you can't have it, you have to take care of business, you have to eliminate all your faults and evil ways. How many lifetimes will it take you to be 'perfect as your Father in heaven is perfect?'

"Mankind certainly has its work cut for them," Adam concluded. "I wish the common Christian belief were true, that all we have to do is live a good life, go to church once a week and then we'll go to heaven when we die. That would be nice and easy."

"You're right, Adam. Unfortunately we have to change ourselves, do the inner work. We have to pluck the weeds out of our garden"

"And all because we've been living ignorantly," Adam stated. "You've mentioned two imperfections, Harish. What are the meanings of those six others?"

Harish explained them as follows: Attachment is dwelling on pleasure and not using discrimination to find out whether the pleasure is good or harmful to us. Because we are attached to pleasure we rationalize that it is good though it may be quite harmful. Repulsion is when we distort the sense of right and wrong, and good and evil. This creates the dual opposites of likes and dislikes. As a result, we avoid what we should do because we find it unpleasant to do so. Body attachment is when we cling to mortal life. This leads to a fear

120

of death, selfishness, greed, possessiveness, and a storing up of earthly treasures thinking this will be our permanent home. Karma is material action that's instigated by egotistic desire. These actions produce binding effects. Christ said 'with what ye measure so shall it be handed out to ye.' We are responsible for all actions; there's no escape from their consequences be it now or hereafter. Habits are the impressions made on the mind by past thoughts and actions that create strong tendencies to repeat themselves. Bad habits bind us to this earth and make us repeat the same mistakes. Latent desires are the unfulfilled desires that remain with us after death. Desire is whatever binds the soul to matter and makes us forget God. If there's no end of desire there's no end of rebirth.

"So there they are, Adam. Keep your eyes and ears open. You'll find the eight imperfections everywhere. But enough of this, let's go spend some time at the springs.

The two friends gathered up the leftovers of their lunch, picked up their packs and resumed the hike. It was past mid-afternoon. The day had become hotter, its heat bearing down on them as they walked in the open desert. Soon they reached the springs; they went to the largest pond, squatted near its edge, and then splashed its cool water onto their face, neck and arms. After they were done they explored the rest of the area. The springs were a series of small ponds lying between two canyon walls. Upon reaching the last one, they sat in the shade around it, talked awhile, then silently left the area and began the trek back to Harish's car.

The returning hike was a study in contrasts. Harish walked the path of a warrior, Adam that of a novice. Harish was a seeker, an explorer after truth. Adam was a novice explorer, a seeker walking only briefly on truth's pathway. Harish had traveled further along that pathway. He was aware of his inner self and tried at all times to remain open to it. He sought a balance between his inner and outer worlds. He had learned long ago that this earth was but a testing ground, a place for learning lessons, growing, and seeking perfection. He sought peace, happiness and love. In the knowledge he had gained, he had come to know that the drunkard drank because he was seeking this same peace, happiness and love. The difference between Harish and the drunkard, the drug addict, the sex addict, and the power hungry dictators of the world, was the balance kept between inner and outer worlds, the soul, and the body and its ego.

"Harish, please pullover over by that grocery store," Adam asked him. "I want to get some flowers for Taneka."

"Are you trying to win her over?" Harish asked.

"Sort of, what do you mean by that?"

"She appeared to be upset when we left the party last night."

"Oh, that, it was really nothing. I'm trying to put everything in its proper place."

"I'll wait in the car for you."

Adam went into the store, found a dozen red roses in the flower section, and bought them.

"Nice choice," Harish told him when he returned to the car. "Taneka will be pleased. Let's get you back home now. Are you going over to her place tonight?"

"Absolutely."

They pulled out of the parking lot and, after a short drive, arrived at Adam's apartment.

"Thanks for the outing today, Harish, it was an interesting time. You've left me with a lot to think about."

"I'm glad you enjoyed it. Please say hello to Taneka for me."

"I shall do that."

Adam grabbed the flowers and his hiking pack and went on into his apartment. He placed the pack on the shelf in the hall closet by the front door then walked into the kitchen and set the roses on the counter. In need of a container, and lacking a vase of any kind, he found an empty quart bottle in the cupboard above him. He went over to the kitchen faucet and filled the bottle about a third of the way up. Then he carefully arranged the roses within it. Satisfied with his work, he pulled out his cell phone and called Taneka.

"Hi, Tan, it's Adam. How's your day been?"

"Okay, I haven't done much. Basically, I've been resting up after last night."

"I have something for you," he stated. "How about if I bring over some Chinese food for dinner, Tan?"

"Chinese sounds good. When will you be here?"

"I need to clean up first. I'll see you in about an hour."

Adam called in the order for Chinese food after he and Taneka were finished talking. He set his cell phone down on the kitchen counter, went into the living room, and glanced out the front window. Camelback Mountain and Demaya's castle were still visible in the day's waning light. He looked at it briefly, sighed, and then headed for the bathroom. * * *

Adam placed the take-out bag on the front steps. He hid the roses behind his back and rang the doorbell. Quickly, he bent down and grabbed the bag. Taneka opened the door. Adam leaned forward and kissed her. "Here's our dinner," he said handing her the takeout bag.

She took it from him and he followed her into her apartment.

"Sit down, Adam. I'll set out the plates and silverware."

Taneka went over to the cabinets. Adam seized the moment and placed the hidden roses on the kitchen table.

"What's this?" She asked returning with the dinnerware.

"It's a peace offering," he answered.

"What for?"

"It's for last night, Tan. I want to set things right between us."

"Your sweet," she declared, went next to him, and kissed him on the cheek.

"I sort of got out of hand. I don't know why."

"It was the tempo of the evening. Stewart's party was pretty wild."

"Harish had a handle on things and helped us regain our senses."

"Where did you two go today?"

"We went to one of his favorite hiking spots in the Superstitions. It was a nice day. We hiked then had lunch and talked."

"What did you talk about?"

"Well, you know Harish, it wasn't about baseball."

"Spiritual, huh?"

"Yep. He told me about man's eight imperfections."

"Was that interesting?"

"Harish made it so. He doesn't try to force his ideas and beliefs on you. That would definitely turn me off. He's an interesting guy. He questions his experiences and is always trying to improve himself."

"What did you get out of this?"

"I don't know. I'm still trying to digest what he said."

"It sounds like Harish planned it that way. He likes helping people."

"He told me that we can't change a person, we can only change ourselves."

"That's true."

"As I've said, he's not pushy about his beliefs. He knows when to stop. He's what a friend should be."

"And what about me?"

"Ditto."

"Ditto? Am I *just* a friend to you, Adam?"

"By the way you say the word *just*, I see you have a deeper meaning. Tan you are my friend and my lover. You are my other half, together we make a whole."

"Ah, that's better, Adam. You're really winning me over now. First you bring flowers and now you flatter me with your words. What's next on your agenda?"

"Food! I'm hungry."

"Food! You're so romantic. You soften me up and then you think only of food."

"Tan, that's because you are food for my soul."

"Nice comeback. Pass the Chow Mein."

Adam and Taneka were two lovers dining on the sunshine of their love. An unseen Hand had lovingly created them, paired them as soulmates, and then sent them out into the world making them rose seeds concealed within the flower's design, and left to grow in the garden of life.

Rose bushes have their flowers and their thorns as Adam and Taneka would soon find out.

Chapter 6

The Boat

"Hey, man, what happened to you Saturday night?" Dinar asked Adam.

"What do you mean?"

"You guys took off with Harish."

Adam pushed himself away from his office desk. "We were tired."

"You missed out on a lot of good stuff."

"What kind of stuff are you referring to?"

"Demaya has a hidden den. He let us in and gave marijuana, opium and cocaine to whoever wanted it."

"Wasn't he concerned about the legal ramifications of that?"

"Demaya sets his own rules, Adam. You should know that by now. Anyway, I tried the opium, and, man," he said excitedly flinging his arm out and dangling his gold bracelet, "I was in a surreal dreamland the rest of the night. Melia drove us home. I don't know how she did it she was so high on grass."

Adam eyed Dinar's jewelry. 'All that glitters is not gold' he thought.

"Dinar, I know you wanted to share this with me but I'm not interested in drugs. I'm a health nut and proud of it. I don't like anything messing with my mind or my body. Is there anything else about Stewart's party you liked besides the hidden den?"

"His magic was phenomenal."

"He knows how to put on a good show. I wonder why he does it."

"I don't know. Anyway, Stewart said our stock purchase is doing well and we'll be cashing in on it soon."

"I could sure use the money. I'll be able to buy my first house."

"I'm investing the dough in my business. Stewart mentioned he might help me out. If it plays out I can open another store. Isn't that great?"

"Does Harish know anything about this?"

"Naw, I haven't told him. I'm waiting for Stewart's finished plans. Well, I've got to go. Melia and I are going shopping."

"What about your workout?"

"I'll pass on it today. Melia's shortening hers to some cardio and some weights. I'm meeting her in the lobby. Catch you later."

Dinar left. Adam picked up his desk phone and made a call.

"Hello, Harish, it's Adam. I saw your cousin a little while ago. Did he tell you what he did after we left the party?"

"He told me about the drugs if that's what you mean."

"I'm worried about him."

"So am I. I've tried giving him advice. He's going to have to learn the hard way what's right and wrong. Pain is a great motivator. It forces us to face our mistakes, and, hopefully, learn our lessons from them."

"It's too bad. I hate seeing him getting caught up in destructive things."

"Adam, I told you to watch out for pitfalls, life is full of them. As you know I'm more than a little leery of Stewart Demaya."

"I'll keep my eyes open, Harish. I appreciate your friendship."

Saturday morning, the first weekend in June, four couples prepared for their boating day. A day's outing out on a refreshing lake offered a break from the summer's heat.

"When are Sam and Jaya picking us up, Rich?"

"In about ten minutes, Des."

"Don't forget to pack the tanning lotion."

"It's in the bag along with our towels and clothing."

Desiree patted him on his back. "You're a good boy, Rich. How do you like my new bikini?"

He gave the bright lemon colored suit a once over. His eyes grew larger.

"Well, do you like the suit?" She asked him.

"The suit's all right. I like what's in it better."

Desiree lit up. "I know, it's the real me you go for," she said teasingly.

"Yeah, it's that great body of yours."

"Which part, my breasts, my legs, my face or what?" She wanted to know.

"It's your whole package, Luv."

Her face broadened into a large smile, her seductive green eyes asking for more. He obliged by swiftly sweeping her into his arms and carrying her into the bedroom.

"Do we have time for this?"

"You know Sam. He's always late."

Richard set her down at the end of bed. The front doorbell rang preventing them from going any farther.

"It looks like Sam's on time. We have to stop," she sighed.

"Oh well, later then, Luv, we'll finish this later."

"I'll be looking forward to it. Don't let me down," she said looking at the bulge in his shorts.

Richard left her and went out and answered the door. "Hi, Sam, I'll get our bag. Desiree will be out shortly. Is there anything I can bring along for you?"

"No, Jaya made sure we have everything."

Desiree entered the room, her bikini clad body now covered with a large T-shirt. "Hi, Sam, where's Jaya."

"She's out in the car waiting for us. Are you ready?"

"As ready as I'll ever be," she answered winking at Richard.

They left the house and walked over to Sam's car parked in the driveway.

"Hi, everyone," Jaya shouted out. She was wearing a false happy face.

Earlier that morning she and Sam had fought. He was upset with her for spending so much time in front of the mirror. She reacted to his comment by pointing out his bad habit of always being late. She told him he had no right to criticize her. She had a right to look nice and it was always worth the extra time to do so. This only added fuel to his fire. He snapped back saying she didn't need the heavy facial makeup and the sprayed stiff hair. She responded by saying he smoked too much and needed to take better care of himself. His final words to her were complaints concerning her attachment to cosmetics and everything else. That was the end of their conversation. When she was ready they got into their car and drove off in an unsettled restlessness. And that is why Jaya was currently wearing her happy face.

"We're off then. We're going to have a fun day," Jaya told everyone with a token half-smile.

The Karnan's boat, moored to the main dock, rested in the lake's stillness. There was a bright sun reflecting off the waters next to it. In the distance a half dozen boats cruised on the lake.

"Don't worry, Ray, I'm almost done."

"You should be. Why do you spend so much time cleaning this boat, Vicki?"

"Because I like a clean boat."

"If you spent half as much time keeping up our house it would be the envy of the neighborhood."

"Cleaning the house is a pain in the ass," Vicki responded.

"Just because you don't like it doesn't mean you shouldn't do it," Ray claimed.

She got hot with him. "Well, you're attached to your cars and girlie magazines."

"I'm attached to these? What about your jewelry? You're always showing that ring off," he snapped back.

"What's that supposed to mean?" She shouted back at him.

"It means you always want fancy things around you. It seems there's no way to satisfy your hunger for them."

"You've got your stuff too. I don't see anything wrong with my jewelry. In fact I'm planning on getting matching earrings and necklace. Don't I deserve them?"

"All right, all right you win," he cried out. "You work hard. You've earned the right to buy whatever you like. I apologize."

"Thank you for admitting my rights. I accept your apology."

Just then they heard a car driving down the road. They turned and watched it come to the dock and park in front of it.

"Our guests have arrived," Vicki announced.

"It's Sam's car. Hey, guys, over here!" Ray yelled out waving his arms.

The two couples stepped out of the car. The men removed their bags and the women made their way to the moored boat.

"Where are Adam and Taneka?" Vicki asked.

"They're coming in their own car," Desiree answered.

The men walked over to the boat.

"You go on and help the women and I'll take care of your bag, Sam."

"All right, Rich, if you insist."

"Welcome aboard everyone," Vicki yelled out. "We can sit back here and wait for the arrival of Adam and his lady friend."

"Stewart wants us to give special attention to Adam and Taneka," Desiree told them. "He likes them, especially Adam. He's got plans for him."

"He seems like a decent enough guy to me," Sam remarked.

"He should be a valuable asset for Universal Holdings," Richard reported.

"We can use him. He has within him the ability to attract others into the fold," Desiree added.

"The more the merrier I always say," Jaya declared.

"Ray, what have you planned for us today?" Richard asked.

"It's going to be an enjoyable outing. We've got lots of food and beer. We can swim, sun, ski, or fish if we like."

"There's a car coming down the road now," Vicki reported.

"It must be them," Richard said. "I'll give them a hand."

Adam drove his Tahoe up next to Sam's car.

Richard left the boat and went over to greet him. "Glad you could make it," he said.

"Thanks, we are too," Adam answered.

"Can I help you with anything?"

"Adam can handle it, Rich," Taneka told him.

Once everybody was aboard Vicki undid the boat from its moorings. Ray went to the helm and started the engines. He let them warm up, then put them into gear and steered the vessel out into the lake. He traveled a ways past the lake's other boats and then put the engines into neutral. Vicki went up to him, they spoke a few words and she returned to the guests. Once again Ray had them under way, this time heading north towards the farthest point of the lake. After thirty-five minutes he cut the two motors and let the vessel coast.

"This is as good a place as any to hangout," he declared.

"Aren't you going to throw out your anchors?" Taneka asked him.

"It wouldn't do any good, it's three hundred feet deep here," he told her. "We'll just let her drift. Since there's no wind today the mild current won't carry us far."

"How long is Roosevelt Lake?"

"It's twenty-two miles long but meanders for about forty miles," he informed her. "There are also several miles of beaches."

"Now I see why a boat this size is useful on this lake," Taneka admitted.

"How's the fishing here?" Adam asked.

"It's quite good actually. There are large bass, some catfish and crappie."

"Is everyone ready to eat?" Vicki burst out.

"I could go for a cold beer along with my food," Richard let known.

Vicki went over to an ice chest by the cabin, removed a six pack and began handing cans of beer out.

"No thanks," Adam said when it was his turn. "Taneka and I'll have lemonade or the like if you have it."

"Ray, Adam's a health nut. I think he's also turning Taneka into one," Desiree exclaimed.

Adam chuckled. "You're right. We rarely drink. Our bodies feel better that way. Besides, it clouds our minds."

"Oh, you like staying in control of yourselves. But your safe with us, come on and live it up," Desiree told them.

"We can live it up without drinking, Desiree," Taneka asserted. "Personally I find enjoyment just being out in nature."

"Yes, of course. But life is full of its adventures."

"Here's to that," Richard cried out raising his beer.

"How about some of that delicious food we've made?" Vicki asked all of them.

"I'm ready any time, any time at all," Sam declared.

Ray sat down next to Taneka and gave her a once over. "Have you lived in Arizona very long?" He asked her.

"Taneka's from back east and relatively new to the area," Adam answered for her.

"Is that right," Ray said. "And how do like it here?"

"It's different," she responded."

"I've lived here several years. Vicki's from Las Vegas, that's where we first met. Stewart transferred her to Phoenix three years ago. In Vegas she worked in one of his subsidiary businesses as a head of customer relations. She's in the same position here. The only difference now is that Vicki oversees all of Universal Holdings' customer relations departments. I'm an accountant and I handle Stewart's bookkeeping."

"Certainly you can't be Stewart's only accountant?" Adam asked.

"No, that would be impossible. Universal Holdings is much too large for that. What I mean is that I oversee the accounting department."

"And you and Vicki are on his board of directors," Taneka confirmed.

"You've met all eight of us now. Stewart is, of course, the chairman of the board. He's the one that calls the shots; after all it's his show. The rest of us have to answer to him. Don't misunderstand me. We each have a field of expertise and we all have a certain amount of freedom. He sees to that. But in the end we have to answer

135

to Demaya. Actually he's quite a good boss. He pays us well and provides us with life's pleasures. I don't think any of us could easily leave him."

"What is Ashley Karmas to him?" Adam wanted to know.

"She's like his right hand man, only in this case I should say right hand woman. Ashley's the vice-president of Universal Holdings as well as head of the legal department. She oversees contract negotiations and makes sure all laws are followed. Everything needs to be in order. Demaya runs a tidy and efficient ship. He expects everyone to operate under the laws that keep the operation running smoothly. He and Ashley have to hold everyone accountable for their actions or the operation would cease to exist. So, for Demaya, everything must fit within the reality of his world. That's why he calls it Universal Holdings."

"That's interesting, Ray, thanks for the insight," Taneka said.

"Can I get you anything else to drink besides juice, Adam?" Ray asked.

"No thanks, I'll be fine with just that,"

"How about you, Taneka?"

"Likewise."

"Very well. Enjoy yourselves," Ray said and then stood up and went to the nearby helm.

"Do you mind if I join you?" Desiree was by them.

"Not at all, Desiree, please sit down," Adam told her.

"I couldn't help overhearing part of your conversation. Are you interested in the directors?"

"It gives Tan and me some insight into Stewart's operation."

"What's your position in the business, Desiree?" Taneka inquired.

"Me," she said laughing, "well, you probably aren't going to believe this, but I'm the one that keeps our sales going. I have a marvelous knack of finding out what our customers want. I'm good at marketing. I make our product line appear to be endless. Advertising is another of my specialties. My ads create strong desires for our product. I'm fresh as a daisy when it comes to finding new items of material desire."

"Where does Richard fit in?" Adam asked her.

"He's Stewart's recruiter. Rich works closely with me. I search out what the public wants and then find the product and Rich promotes it. His athletic background opens customer's doors. Stewart once helped Richard clear his public name over some scandal. Stewart changed any misunderstanding the public had for Rich. Stewart's marketing created Rich's good guy image. He's become a masterful recruiter. He's very powerful in promoting Universal Holdings. Is there anything else you'd like to know, Adam?"

"At the moment I can't think of anything."

"Well, I say let's all go in for a swim then," Desiree shouted out loudly for all to hear.

"I'll steer us closer to shore," Ray told them. He started the engines once more. "We'll go close to a beach. If anybody wants to hang out on shore they can."

Ray cruised within twenty feet of the shore and cut the engines. He and Vicki each went to each end of the vessel and each dropped an anchor.

"Why are there two anchors?" Adam wanted to know.

"That's so the boat doesn't swirl and stays in one place," Taneka answered.

"That's right, you remember well," Ray said winking at her.

Desiree pulled off her T-shirt. "I'm going in," she announced loudly.

Ray stared at her scarcely clad body. "Nice body, I like what your showing."

"Put your tongue back in your mouth and stop drooling," Vicki cried out.

Adam and Taneka looked at one another and laughed to themselves.

Desiree jumped into the water and then Richard followed her.

"How is it?" Sam shouted out to them.

"Refreshing," Richard claimed.

"Do you want to go in, Tan?" Adam inquired.

"Not yet. But when I do I'd like to swim to the beach."

Jaya and Vicki went over to the side of the boat and looked down at the water. Richard was swimming after Desiree who was playing hard to get.

"Jaya," Vicki said, "I've been admiring your diamond. It must've cost a bundle."

"Sam knew he had to pay a bunch for this ring if he ever was going to catch me."

"And you took the bait."

"It's actually a promise ring. It's hard to get any commitments out of Sam. Would you like to try it on?"

"It's a lot like mine," Vicki said holding up her wedding ring."

"We both like our like diamonds."

Jaya removed her ring and then handed it to Vicki. Their hands met awkwardly and the ring slipped away. Both grabbed for it but their efforts failed and the ring fell into the water.

"My precious diamond!" Jaya yelled at the top of her lungs while leaning over the edge of the railing. She lost her balance, fell out of the boat, hit head hard against its side, and then disappeared within the water.

"She can't swim!" Sam shouted out. "She can't swim!"

"I'll get her," Adam claimed and jumped over the railing.

"Richard help him!" Sam yelled down at him.

Richard swam over to where Jaya had gone down. He and Adam both went under the water together. What seemed like minutes passed, and then they, along with Jaya appeared on the surface. Jaya was panting heavily and in a full state of panic.

"Take her there," Ray commanded pointing to the stern.

They pulled Jaya to the swim platform at the end of the boat. Ray and Sam helped lift her up onto its wooden ledge.

"I don't want to die," she said, "I don't want to die," she repeated shaking from head to foot.

"You'll be all right, Darling, you'll be all right," Sam said trying to reassure her.

"Vicki's in the water!" Desiree suddenly yelled out. In the confusion nobody had noticed that Vicki had jumped in the lake in search of the ring.

"Are you all right?" Ray shouted out to her.

She looked up at him, shook the water from her face and red, stringy hair, and then snapped back at him, "Of course I'm not all right; Jaya's damn ring is gone!"

139

"We'll deal with that later. Come back in."

Vicki climbed up into the boat. "Give me that towel over there," she demanded. Ray handed it to her. She wiped off her head and slender body.

"You're responsible for losing my ring! I want it replaced!" Jaya yelled at Vicki.

"What does she mean?" Vicki asked Sam.

"It's the diamond ring, Vicki; she's blaming you for dropping it into the lake."

"I'm so sorry Jaya. It was an accident. Please don't be angry."

"I want my ring back!" She shouted angrily.

Sam intervened. "Look, dear, you never really had control of the ring."

"Don't try defending her. Are you going to buy me another diamond like that one or are you going stop being wishy-washy and demand she replace it?"

"Listen, Jaya, I don't like your attitude. I told you I'd take care of things."

Jaya appeared to cool down somewhat. "Well do it then," she ordered him and then went over to their travel bag and removed her purse. She opened it and took out a diamond bracelet. "I want the new ring to exactly match this."

"Let's go back to having a good time," Ray told everyone. "Does anyone want to go to the beach or use an inner tube for floating on the lake?"

"I've had enough of the water," Jaya responded. "I want to go home now."

"Now wait a minute," Sam said. "There are other people to consider here, Jaya."

Her unsettled eyes glared at him. "I don't care."

Sam shrugged his shoulders and sighed. "I guess you better take us in, Ray. What about you guys?" He asked Richard and Desiree.

"We can leave any time," Richard said standing up for him.

"That's right, Sam, we'll go with you," Desiree told him.

"That's settled then," Rich announced. "Ray, take us back to the dock. How about you two?" He asked turning to Adam and Taneka.

"We'll go with the flow," Adam answered.

Ray went to the controls and started the engines. Then he and Vicki pulled up the anchors and soon they were underway for the docks.

"That was sure some incident, Adam," Taneka voiced quietly.

"I know. It took the wind out of the sails, pun intended," he joked.

"I believe we've just seen a few of the eight imperfections Harish told you about."

"I think your right, Tan."

"So what do we do now, head back home?"

"I'll do whatever you want."

Ray sped up the boat. A half hour later they were at the starting point of the day's journey. The boat was secured to the dock. Sam and Jaya stepped out onto the wooden planks.

Richard handed Sam his bag. "I'll get ours, and then Desiree and I will meet you at your car. Thanks, Ray and Vicki for the trip today such as it was."

"We'll see you Monday at the office," Ray conveyed.

Sam and Ray left with their partners.

"What's your pleasure?" Ray asked Adam and Taneka after they were gone.

"We can hang around for a few more hours. I'd like to see the rest of the lake if you don't mind," Adam answered.

"Then if you ladies will undo the lines will be off again. Adam, sit down next to me and we'll discuss old times."

Ray steered them once more out on the lake. "Adam, we'll check out the dam then go to the northern end of the lake."

Adam examined him as they traveled along. Ray was slenderer now. It was obvious that his attachment to the pleasures of life had taken its toll on his body. Such are his ways Adam reasoned. Putting these thoughts aside Adam asked, "Ray, you've earned a degree in accounting?"

Ray gazed back at the stern. The women were in their bikinis sunning themselves. "Adam, I like figures," he said. "It took me an extra year to get that accounting degree. After graduating I worked in an accountant's office then ended up in one of my own."

"Then you met Stewart and he set you up in his business. How long did it take to become a director?"

"Two years. I worked my way up to chief accountant and the head of the department. It's been very rewarding," Ray claimed.

"Have you managed to put money away?"

"Yes. Stewart awards us when we perform well. I'll be getting a nice bonus this summer and another in December, that's Stewart's way. I'm going to buy a bigger boat soon."

"Why, doesn't this one fit your needs?"

"Adam, I'll have the money, so why not get something bigger and better? You'll have to come by sometime and see my car collection, I think you'll be impressed."

"Cars, how many do you have?"

"Right now I have five in my collection and I'm still counting. They're vintage sports cars. Storing them is another matter. Thank goodness I've got a large piece of land."

"Where do you live?"

"In East Mesa."

"Do you ever see Harish?" Adam asked changing the subject.

"No, just Dinar. Harish and I still don't see eye-to-eye. You know how he is, always concerned about doing the right thing and all that. Dinar and I hang out from time to time. We both enjoy life's pleasures. Harish takes life too seriously. I'm here to get the most out of it and whatever desire strikes me I go for it. Why not?"

Adam made no reply and instead watched the passing scenery. This, Adam thought, is what he enjoyed most. Nature and its ongoing variety gave him satisfaction. That's not to say, he realized, that there were some things he would like to own. If his investment with Stewart paid off big, his house dream would be realized. Heck, maybe he would even have enough cash left over to buy some other things.

"Adam!" Taneka called out to him. "Come and join us back here."

"Duty calls, we'll talk again later," he explained to Ray leaving him at the wheel.

"Vicki's still upset about the ring, Adam," Taneka began, "I don't think Jaya should blame her for losing it. It was an accident. It shouldn't stand between friends."

"That's right," Vicki snapped out. "I'm pissed at her for acting the way she did. I don't like it one bit," she added hotly.

Adam mused over her words, wondering if there was a connection between her actions and her red hair, and then dismissed the idea. "I'm sure you two can work things out and the right thing will be done."

"That woman can be a real bitch," Vicki claimed then began telling them about Jaya's other shortcomings.

"Vicki, I don't want to hear this. If you're going to speak of other's faults you should begin with yours," Taneka told her.

Vicki's face hardened and she looked away.

Adam stepped in. "Vicki, tell me more about your position at Universal Holdings."

Vicki quieted down. "All right," she said. "As customer relations and personnel director, I help maintain our staff and see that everything goes according to Stewart's wishes. He's particular about his business and is good at overseeing it. He should be, he's done it for I don't know how many years."

"How old is Stewart?" Taneka wondered.

"Nobody really knows," Vicki answered. "That's part of his mystique. He reveals only what he wants to. Anyway, what does it matter as long as we are all taken care of?"

Adam and Taneka shrugged their shoulders. There was so much loyalty and mystery surrounding Stewart Demaya. It made Adam wonder just where he fit into Stewart's plans and if those plans would ever affect his relationship with Taneka.

"I don't care what you say, Sam, I want my ring back. I'm going to get it one way or another," Jaya declared, her dark eyes fierce with anger.

They were still traveling in the car about halfway to their home from the lake. Richard and Desiree were in the backseat listening to the couple argue.

Sam lit a cigarette and opened the car window slightly. "Honey, you're taking this too seriously. I'll get you another ring if that will please you."

"Open your window wider, don't smoke us all out," she ordered.

"Hey, you two, I've got a great idea about that ring," Richard spoke out. "I know how it can be replaced without any cost to you."

"At no cost?" Sam wondered. "Really and how are we going to do that?"

"Yeah, how are we going to do that?" Jaya repeated.

"Next weekend we'll all go to Vegas," Richard told them.

Sam's eyes lit up. "That's an excellent idea my friend, an excellent idea. What do you think, Jaya? We could use the vacation. You and Des can do your thing and Rich and I will do ours and in between we'll be together."

"I think it's just an excuse for you to indulge in one of your bad habits."

"Jaya, we'll have a great time. I'll buy you a ring and matching earrings."

Jaya smiled to herself. More jewelry, clothing or whatever would suit her just fine. She loved owning new things. That's probably why Stewart put her in charge of purchasing at Universal Holdings. It was a job she was well suited for.

"So what do you say, Jaya," Richard said. "Do you want to go?"

"Come on, girl, we'll have a ball or maybe two," Desiree told her.

"Okay, I'm in, but just you remember, Sam, what you promised. And don't lose any money at those crap tables you like to play so much."

"Don't worry about that, Luv, don't worry about that. I'm going to win us a bundle."

"I've heard that before," Jaya told him.

Chapter 7

Imperfections

Adam and Taneka were playing their game, sending notes back and forth to one another on their laptops. Adam sent the first one.

Like a gentle breath of bliss, like a silent river moving beneath the sands, that is what your love is to me.

Taneka replied.

Enhance that breath and send it back to me. Breathe thy eternal love throughout this mortal frame of mine.

Adam answered.

This new breath I breathe out shall unite us. Together we dip our love into the silent river moving beneath the sands of our existence.

Taneka sent back:

We must drink the cup of our love quickly – Harish and your sister are at my door. We will be there shortly. I will allow you to take me home later.

Love and kisses to you.

Tan

Adam laughed then turned off his computer. He went to the bedroom, changed clothes, and then went back out to the kitchen. He opened the refrigerator, removed a pizza, and then placed it next to the oven. The salad would be left up to the women. With that settled he went into the living room and turned on the television. A short time later his three guests arrived.

"Come on in," he said opening the door wide for them. The guests stepped in. He hugged Taneka.

"I'd like a hug too, Brother," Edwina requested.

"Shall do," he responded and wrapped his arms around her.

"What about me?" Harish kidded him. They shook hands.

"I've got the pizza ready to go into the oven. You girls can make the salad, if you don't mind," Adam told them.

A half hour later they were at the table enjoying their meal.

"Yum, this is good pizza, Adam," Taneka spoke out. "Where did you find it?"

"At the health food market, the crust is made from whole wheat pastry flour and the pizza has five kinds of cheeses. I worked hard on it, you know."

"That would be the day," Edwina declared. "You do about as much cooking as I lift weights," she added and then chuckled.

"What do you mean, Sis? Don't you know Tan has been helping with my meals? She's a great cook."

"How was that boating day for you two?" Harish asked them.

Taneka told him what had happened at Lake Roosevelt.

"That's interesting," Edwina said. "Harish, you know more about those people than we do. What are your thoughts?"

"They're different. They tend to be too worldly. Ray, of course, I knew in India. We more or less grew up together there. He's drawn to serving his senses and seeking pleasure. Unfortunately, he's steered Dinar in the same direction."

"What's wrong with pleasure?" Adam wanted to know.

"Nothing if you find it in the right places. The problem with Ray is that he's gone overboard in his quest for it. He lacks discrimination, thus has no balance. That's why he and Dinar get along so well. They both want more sex, money, and material things. They believe this will give them happiness; instead it's just created a need for something bigger and better. Their thirsts for them never end."

"Harish, Edwina told me that you've practiced meditation since you were a child," Taneka stated.

"Yes, that's right."

"How do you meditate?" Taneka asked.

"Do you mean the posture or the technique?"

"Edwina and I know the meditation posture, I was thinking of the technique."

"Let me show you the posture for Adam's sake." Harish climbed down from his chair and sat on the floor. He crossed his legs,

149

straightened his back, and placed his upturned hands at the junction between his thighs and abdomen. His eyes were upturned and closed.

"This is the lotus posture. You don't have to be in this posture for meditation. What's important is that your spine is kept straight and is free from restrictions. Focus your eyes and your attention at the place between the eyebrows. This is referred to as your third eye or spiritual eye."

"Why is this important?" Adam wanted to know.

"Because the spiritual eye is the center of concentration. Focusing at that point draws your attention away from the body and its senses. If your back is bent your nerves become constricted and your attention is drawn to the body. This is somewhat true when your spine is resting against the back of a chair or back support. It's difficult to have lengthy meditations because your mind will most likely end up being drawn into body awareness. Why don't we all try to meditate now?"

"I'm not going to sit here cross-eyed and cross-legged!" Adam exclaimed.

Harish slapped his thighs and fell over on the floor in a fit of hilarity. The women laughed with him.

"What's so funny?" Adam asked them.

"Brother," Edwina answered, "your eyes are not crossed-eyed. Your eyes are just upturned and concentrated at the point between the eyebrows."

"Oh, I thought they naturally became cross-eyed, that's all."

Harish sat back up. "Let's begin again. Adam, one may meditate while seated in a chair. One doesn't have to be cross-legged and, of course, one is not cross-eyed. People who pray deeply find that they naturally keep a straight spine and that their concentration is focused at the spiritual eye. You see, deep prayer is really meditation. Any prayer that's done without concentration isn't really prayer; it's just a mental repetition of words. It's an absence of the mind; there's no power in the prayer. The Christian mystics all prayed in a deeply, concentrated, meditative state. Mechanical words have no value."

"And that's true meditation?" Taneka asked.

"Yes," Harish responded, "a fully focused mind with the spine erect are absolutely necessary for success in meditation. Jesus said 'if thine eye be single thy whole body shall be full of light.' He was referring to our spiritual or third eye. Mystics throughout the ages have referred to the deep meditative states or experiences as Ecstatic Communion, Ecstasy, Bliss, Supreme Joy, Samadhi, and Nirvana. So you see the world's true religions each have their own term for that supreme experience found in meditation."

"What about meditation techniques?" Taneka asked.

"Meditation techniques are scientific. The goal is to shut off the six senses and to become fully concentrated on the Object of your meditation."

"How would a beginner like me meditate?" Adam wished to know.

"One would simply go into the meditated posture, focus his attention at the spiritual eye located between the eyebrows, and pray to God in the language of his heart. One could also try visualizing a great saint or Master such as Jesus and pray to him. Another practice would be to try and feel an aspect of God such as love, peace, joy or wisdom and then try to become one with that aspect." * * *

After the lengthy meal the two couples watched a movie chosen by Harish. He and Edwina left shortly after it ended. The movie they had viewed was titled *Spring, Summer, Fall, Winter, ... Spring.* It was about a young boy who is taken to a monk's retreat located by a small lake within a mountain forest. The monk is the boy's spiritual teacher and, as such, comes to learn his student's weaknesses. When the boy reaches puberty a teenage girl is brought to the retreat. His passions are aroused and he seduces the girl. His restlessness and newly formed desires turns him to the outside world. He leaves his teacher and the peace and tranquility of the retreat for the material offerings of the world. Years later he returns.

He has committed a serious crime. His life has fallen into decadence and disarray. He seeks a return to the peace and contentment he had known in his youth. Unfortunately, his actions and bad habits have taken a firm hold upon him. By the time two police officers arrive at the retreat to arrest him he has come to realize that the happiness he sought in the material world only has given him misery and a life of mental anguish.

"Leave it to Harish to have chosen that movie," Taneka commented. "I think he must've planned this evening well, first with the dinner discussion and then this movie."

"That's Harish, Tan. He looks into life's deeper meanings. He wants to learn from his or others' experiences. What did you think of the movie?"

"It was appropriate. It gave us a good example of why we shouldn't expect joy from temporal things. It helped me to understand what Harish has been telling us."

"I see."

"And," Taneka went on, "it helped put our relationship into a new perspective."

"A new perspective?"

"Yes, Adam, we are together for a reason. Our relationship is not one to be ruled by our senses. We both want to achieve the same lofty goals."

"I know what you're driving at."

"You better, or else we don't have a relationship."

"Tan, you know that loving you is my heart's desire."

"And mine for you is my soul's delight," she added.

They both laughed. Their romantic game had grown into an intuitive knowledge of one another's thoughts.

"So this is where we are now," Adam mused.

Taneka snuggled against him. "I've been looking for you all my life. Promise me that we'll always be together and that nothing will ever divide us."

"You have my word, Tan. Ever since I reached adolescence I've looked for someone to share lives with, to grow old together, to search and find life's riddles with. And now I've found you. You are the answer to my unsaid prayers."

His words brought tears to her eyes and his became misty. They kissed with passion, their senses aroused with desire. She pulled her lips away.

"Should we?" She asked him.

He felt the brightness of her eyes touching his. "It won't be lust, Tan, this time it will be love," he declared.

"I don't want ever again to feel what we did in Demaya's garden."

"What we felt? I thought it was just me lusting for you."

"I wanted you in that way," she confessed meekly.

"You had lust for me? Is that why you pulled away so suddenly?"

"Partly so. I was overcome by it all. Demaya's party, his hypnotic effect on everyone, and the suddenness of our uncontrolled passions were overwhelming me. But we couldn't have sex there. The environment and our motives were all wrong."

Taneka was right on all counts, Adam thought. Something, the world, Stewart Demaya, their deeply rooted desires, any and all of them was playing havoc with their emotions at that party. And here they were now openly discussing what they had felt and almost succumbed to. He did want Taneka sexually but he would never have her in an uncontrolled way. He had too much love and respect for her.

"Do you think if we make love now it will be like the boy in the movie we just saw? Do you think we'll be creating more worldly desires for ourselves?" He asked her.

She answered him. "If it's part of our greater love for one another then it must have its place. But we have to realize that it's just a place, the steppingstone of our growth into a pure and unconditional love."

"You have wisdom about you tonight, Tan. We still have much to learn. I want us to grow old together in our gained knowledge."

"We mustn't misuse our time. We have to complete this journey," she let him know then said, "Not a day goes by that I'm not thinking of you, Thomas Adam Langston."

They kissed once more; each gave the other a longing for oneness.

"To release ourselves fully now is still sex," she claimed when the kiss ended.

"I know. I also know that it brings us closer together. Don't you feel that?"

"More to love, yes. We're using our steppingstone to greater love."

"I like the steppingstone."

"Just you remember, this isn't a substitute for what we are or for what we want to become," she pointed out.

"I'll remember," he uttered.

Their words ended. They gazed again deeply into each other, and then they melt, commingled their feelings and longings, into a wholeness of their beings. They went into the bedroom, removed their clothes, and stood naked before the dresser's mirror. They were like children gazing at each other in wonderment.

"Adam,' Taneka said, "I want to touch it."

"No," he said.

"Why not?" She asked.

"Because you've already broken yours off."

She giggled, ignored his warning, grabbed a hold of the part she was missing, and pulled him onto the bed with her.

Two young lovers found joy in their physical oneness. This was their beginning. They knew that in their growth there would be other ways of expressing what they were becoming. Harish was part of this. He was helping them break through the surface of their soul's encased walls. They were miners using the pickaxe of love and friendship to chip and break away their souls' coating, which, once done, would reveal its diamond brilliance. Little did they know that hidden within that diamond was the Mother Lode.

Adam left the gym floor and went on into the locker room. Richard Eagleton was sitting solemnly in front of a mirror. He was staring at the scar made by the surgeon who had put his leg back together after the *NFC* championship game two years earlier.

"I have to hand it to you, Rich," Adam said moving near him. "You are one tough guy to be able to walk again normally. It's like nothing had ever happened to your leg."

Richard sat up. Sadness was written all over him. "Johnny Ortiz took his life yesterday."

"That name sounds familiar. Who was he?"

"He was my teammate. I had an affair with his wife."

"Yes, I remember now."

"They were just going through a divorce. I guess he couldn't handle it. Do you ever wish you could undo your past, Adam?"

"There are some things I would like to change."

"It's my damn desires for women. I can't break the habit," Richard said shaking his head. "I guess you really don't know how your actions affect others. It takes something like this to wake you up, doesn't it?"

Adam didn't know what to say. Before him he was seeing an example of the destructive powers of a harmful habit. Richard was a victim of his uncontrolled appetite. His habit had imprisoned him. It had become an unquenchable desire grown into destructive action. Richard, Adam realized, was not just a super ego ex-jock, a super macho man made of steel. He was another human being imprisoned by one of man's imperfections.

"I'm really sorry for you, Rich. You've got to just go on, put the past behind you. Don't dwell on it and learn from your mistakes."

"You're right, of course, but damn it's hard," he replied, his face tightening. "It's going to take more than this to bring me down, man. I've got my life and my friends to help keep me going."

"Who do you count on the most?"

"Desiree and Sam. The three of us let the good times roll."

"Interesting," Adam expressed.

"We're the interesting trio."

"Didn't all of you go somewhere last weekend?"

"We went to Vegas, you know, Sin City."

"Any luck?"

"Sam and I both scored. Not with the bucks, it was with the women," he told him falling into his usual self. "We went to a couple shows, great bodies by the way. We gambled quite a bit. Sam and I ended up losing money but what the heck we all had fun. Desiree and Jana won some money at the slots, though. They seemed satisfied with that. At least Desiree was happy. Jaya was hoping Sam would win enough money to buy her another diamond ring but that didn't happen. She's still mad at him and Vicki. He told her not to worry about the ring; he would use this summer's bonus money to buy her that new diamond. So that was that. Tell me what you've been up to."

"I'm spending most of my time with Taneka."

"Taneka's a pretty woman, I wouldn't mind hanging out with her."

"You've got, Desiree," Adam said defensively. "You don't need another woman."

"Don't get your feathers up, man. I was just trying to say Taneka's a looker and you're a lucky man."

"Desiree isn't too bad herself. Keep her happy or she might just slip away."

"Don't you worry; I've got what she wants. She needs me as much as I need her."

"Yes, I understand that," Adam divulged. "You two definitely exist for one another. Well, I've got work left to do before I can call it a day."

Adam started to leave. Richard wasn't done. "I didn't mean anything about Taneka. I just meant she's a keeper. You're fortunate to have her."

"Thanks, Rich," Adam said.

"I'd like you to stay a little longer if you don't mind."

Adam sat down next to him. Richard began talking about the other directors and the experience on the boat. He told him not to judge them harshly. They all had their good and bad points. Then he spoke of Harish. He told him Harish means well and has good ideas, even though he didn't understand all of them, he still respected him.

As Richard talked Adam's eyes fell on the mirror next to him. From his vantage point Richard's scarred leg did not appear on the mirror. He glanced back at the physical Richard sitting next to him. The six inch scar on his right leg was clearly visible. To see it or not to see it was just a matter of one's vantage point.

Richard went on talking about his friends and his relationships with Stewart and Desiree. As he rambled on Adam became aware that he was both listening to Richard's words and thinking entirely about something else. Funny that one could do this, he thought, then his mind let that thought slip by and he began thinking about Richard's character. Richard, he reasoned, has some depth. He's, at times, aware of the consequences of his actions. He knows then that he has those two worlds, the inner one, his soul and conscience that help him know his wrongs, and the outer one, his ego, that's controlling him and leading him astray. Yet, in spite of this, he doesn't do anything to correct his faults. He's a helpless victim of his habits and desires.

Adam put that observation aside. Glancing once more at Richard he began analyzing the former athlete's body. It was like a bodybuilder's. A bodybuilder must have five things in order to be successful. These are the five 'S's.' The S's are size, separation, striations, symmetry, and style. Rich's muscles are of good size, are separated so that each individual part of the muscle is clearly distinguishable, his muscle's striations or strands are visible, and his body is completely symmetrical. This means that his body is balanced, in proper proportion, and no one muscle group stands out above another. Even though each muscle is developed properly, and, on its own is quite remarkable, it must not take away from the body as a whole. Certainly Richard has four of the 'S's. The fifth 'S,' style, is determined when the bodybuilding contestant poses on the stage in front of the judges and audience. Where does Richard fit in all this? He does put on a good worldly show. But then there's his scarred leg. A contestant loses points if there are any flaws in his physique. What

159

kind of flaw is Richard showing me now? Does it leave him vulnerable to his inner world, his soul?

"Adam?' Richard asked, "Are you with me buddy?"

Adam broke away from his own thoughts. "Sorry, I was just thinking about what you've said and where it all fits in."

"What things do you mean?"

"Life," Adam answered. "Two worlds, our outer world and our inner world."

"You sound like Harish. Maybe you've been hanging out too much with him," Richard stated half seriously.

"Maybe I have. My life used to be much simpler. Now I'm questioning myself daily. Yet, Harish said life is simple and we make it complex."

Richard glanced at his scarred leg. "I think he's right."

"I've wanted to ask you about Stewart. How well to do you know him?"

"No one knows Stewart well. And if you're going to ask me about his age, the answer is I don't know. I don't think anybody does. Stewart's a mystery man. You feel his presence yet he's in the background controlling everything."

"That's an interesting observation. I noticed there are seven rooms in his castle yet we were allowed to see only six of them."

"That's right. Everybody who enters the castle for the first time does so by way of the second room. We go into the door in the back of building. Stewart likes everybody to move on down to the last, seventh room."

"Has anyone gone back up through the rooms and into the first room?"

"As far as I know it's kept locked. One time at a party a couple of guests somehow got into that room. Then I believe they left. At least I never saw them again at the party. Why are you asking these questions, Adam?"

"I'm just curious. It just seemed strange to me that night. Harish had wandered around a bit and made his way up the hallway next to that room. An attendant saw him there and made him go back down to the party in the red room."

"Harish toured the rainbow rooms."

"That's a good name for them. Well, it's getting late, Rich, and I really have to run. I'll see you later."

Chapter 8

Summer

It is the wind of worldliness that always disturbs the mind which may be likened to a candle flame. If that flame does not flicker then one is said to have attained yoga.

Adam observed the cars, buses and commuter trains flowing constantly along the city's main arteries and cross streets below him. "It's quite a view, Stewart," he said turning away from the window.

"Yes, one sees The Valley for miles." Stewart agreed.

"You can keep an eye on things up here." Dinar claimed.

"Why isn't your office on the top floor?" Adam wished to know.

"That's my private quarters. I use it when I'm needed here or when I return from overseas' business."

Stewart's office was rectangular in shape. In size it was about twenty feet by thirty feet. There was a cherry wood conference table with a dark red and blue Turkish rug beneath it. On top of the table at its center was a large globe perhaps sixteen inches high. At its base was a figure of Atlas holding the world on his shoulders. However, on closer inspection, the figure was actually Stewart Demaya. Someone had cleverly sculptured his likeness. Around the table eight chairs sat in place, their cushioned seats covered with a burgundy and gold satin. Stewart's desk was a matching cherry wood as was all the other room's furniture. On the corner of his desk was a replica of the same globe that was on his table. It was smaller. Hanging on the wall opposite the desk were three classical paintings. The wall to the left had a photo of Universal Holdings' eight directors meeting at Stewart's conference table.

"Please sit by my desk."

Stewart leaned back in his high-backed chair. He opened his desk's center drawer, reached in and came out holding two envelopes. He gave one to Adam and the other to Dinar. "These are for you. Please open them," he requested.

Dinar tore his open. "A check for fifty-six grand! I can't believe it."

"That's your return on the stock investment," Stewart announced. "Why are you hesitant, Adam?"

"I was waiting for Dinar," Adam responded and then opened his. He discovered a check for forty-four thousand and eight hundred dollars. The investment had yielded five and half times its original amount. How did Stewart pull this off?

"Wow, I certainly wasn't expecting this much, Stewart. Thank you." Adam told him.

"Yeah, thanks Stewart," Dinar said after overcoming his initial surprise. "I'm glad I took you up on that offer. I can sure use this money."

"You both are welcome," Stewart said and then grew serious. "Now I have something I want to discuss with both of you. Dinar, you first, have you given any more thought to your business's expansion?"

Dinar rubbed his thumb along his gold wristwatch. "Yes. Unfortunately it will take more money than I have. This check," he said holding it up, "will help but not enough to open another store."

The speckled sunlight coming through the window cast Stewart's face in light and shadow. He gazed intently at the two young men with his dark mysterious eyes. "One store," he exclaimed. "Dinar, we talked about this before. I'm going to lend you the money you need to open a chain of stores. Think big, young man."

"A chain?"

"That's right, a chain. And you," Stewart said turning to Adam, "will oversee a chain of health clubs."

Adam swallowed hard. And like Dinar he asked, "A chain?"

"Yes, a chain," Stewart said emphatically, "You will oversee every one of my Universal Fitness Clubs."

"But, sir, you only have one club."

"Not any more, I've just acquired the California Fitness clubs here in Phoenix. I want you to be my district manager. What do you say to that?"

"I don't know what to say. I'm at a loss for words."

"Don't be," Stewart declared then went on. "I have something else for you. I think you'll find it to your liking." He opened his desk drawer once more and came out with another envelope. It was thicker than the others. He gave it to Adam. "Here, use my letter opener this time."

Adam took the opener from him and with it neatly sliced the envelope open. He found a check which he partially removed. His eyes narrowed. "Twenty thousand dollars, I don't understand. You've already given me my investment's return."

Stewart grinned. A beam of sunlight once more played on his black hair and handsome face. His dark eyes twinkled with shrewdness. Demaya was working his subtle ways. "That's your summer bonus. But that's not all that's in there. Look again."

This time Adam removed the check. There were two folded papers remaining in the envelope. He took them out, unfolded each one, and then read them over. "You want to double my salary plus give me a commission on net sales," he said excitedly.

"Yes, that's right. I want a long term relationship with you."

Adam thought this over. His hand went to the letter opener that he had placed in front of him and he began twirling it absently.

Adam was unsure of the commitment Stewart wanted. Yes, he wanted to grow in the business world. A six-figure salary would give him financial security. He could buy most of the things he desired. That would be nice. But lengthy commitments turned him off. Exclusive of gyms, he had avoided anything representing memberships. This included reading clubs, social clubs, or whatever fell between them. College fraternities had not interested him. He attended few social events, not even his college graduation. He had only gone to his high school ceremony because he was forced to. It was not that he was anti-social. He got along well with people. He was definitely 'people friendly.' He would help another in need. What he mostly disliked was falseness in other's motives and social climbing. His chosen friends did not have a false sense of values.

Now Stewart wanted him to become a long-term member of his organization. Could he do this? What would be expected of him in the long run? How committed did he have to be? He preferred to do things on his own, yet had always been reluctant to go into business for himself. It wasn't the idea of failure that stopped him. It was the total investment of both his time and money. Running another's business meant he wouldn't have to use his money nor would he solely be responsible for the success or failure of the business. This being the case, maybe it was better for him to invest his future with Stewart. After all, it was Stewart's money and Stewart's responsibility for the existence of his business world.

"Your performance has been exemplary, Adam. Ashley will be here shortly. You and Dinar will go with her and work out the contract arrangements. Adam, I want you to be a permanent member of Universal Holdings."

"And you," Stewart said looking firmly at Dinar, "will move into a secure position with Universal Holdings once you've signed your contract."

"Contract? What do you mean, Stewart?" Dinar was still thinking about how he was going to spend his fifty-six grand.

"I mean the funds I'm going to lend you for your chain of stores."

Dinar's mind cleared. "Yes, a chain of stores, that would be nice, but I don't know if I can handle the loan payments."

"Nonsense! The interest rate will be almost negligible and it will be a long term note. You'll easily be able to make those monthly payments to me. Why this deal will make you a fixture within Universal Holdings."

"What about Harish, I don't think he'll go along with this."

The corner of Stewart's mouth constricted. His dark eyes became darker and more intense. "Your cousin's presence, or lack thereof, does cause problems." Stewart sat back, paused briefly, and reflected on what he was going to say next. "Dinar," he continued, "you're worrying about something that we'll easily manage. You can buy Harish out from the funds I advance you. We'll come up with a workable arrangement. Either, way, we'll get along without Harish being in the fold. I will see to that. You and Adam sit tight now. I'll call Ashley. She'll complete the necessary paperwork." His hand went to his phone and he punched in three numbers.

A minute or so passed and then Ashley arrived. She glided into the office. Her high heels accentuated perfectly shaped diamond calves. She wore, as seemed her style, a tightly fitting outfit. It was dark green. Her blond hair framed her stunningly beautiful face. She smiled at the three men with her auburn bedroom eyes and thin lips. "Adam, Dinar, welcome to our team," she said to the two young men.

Nice legs, Adam said to himself standing up to greet her. *Those shoes definitely work to your advantage. Dinar's tongue must be hanging out.*

Dinar also stood up. He had a stupid grin on his face and played with his watch.

"I have the documents ready, Stewart. Adam and Dinar will have to initial the key points and then sign the instrument. When it's said and done all of the legal commitments will be covered," Ashley told him.

"Excellent!" Stewart exclaimed. "Adam and Dinar, please go along with Ashley to her office. She will show you around the

168

building when everything is in order. I'll meet you later at the luncheon that has been arranged for you."

Adam and Dinar followed Ashley out of the room and down the hallway and then into her office. Her room was about two-thirds the size of Stewarts. It had large windows with opened blinds covering them. The furniture was of oak. The entire floor carpeted in beige. In front of the windows was an oak conference table with twelve chairs around it. The table was bare except for a vase in the middle which contained multi-colored flowers. To the right of the table was an oak desk with a matching work station on its left and behind it. The desk was situated in such a way that one sitting there could easily see if someone entered the room. Along the back wall were waist high filing cabinets. On one of them there was a cage containing two hamsters, one of which was inside a wheel. The wheel was going round and round.

"Ashley, I see you like animals," Adam said to her.

'They're like little people," she remarked.

"That's a unique way of seeing them," Adam added.

"We'll sit at the conference table," Ashley requested.

The two men went to the table and sat down. Ashley stepped over to the oak file cabinet underneath the hamsters' cage. She opened the top drawer and brought out two folders. Then she picked up a leather briefcase next to the cage and joined them.

"Adam, we'll start with your contract," she announced while removing it from one of the folders. "Would you like me to read it to you?"

"No, I prefer to do that myself. When I'm finished we'll go over it if need be." Adam told her.

169

"Very well," she said. She handed him the contract "Dinar you might as well read yours now." She placed his in front of him.

Ashley removed duplicates of their contracts from the folders.

"Well, how does it seem?" Ashley asked Adam when he was finished. "Are you ready to sign and make it official?"

"I like everything but its length, Ashley. I would feel more comfortable with a one year deal."

Ashley's face tightened. A fly that had been buzzing around the room tried landing on her nose. She swatted at it. The fly flew away only to return, this time settling on the contract in front of her.

"Adam, why just one year, don't you realize what Stewart is offering you?"

"He's being most generous. I'm just not comfortable with the lengthy commitment."

"Oh, I see," she said straightening up. "You are a cautious one, aren't you? Stewart thought this might be the case. Very well, we'll change the length of time. Are you sure you want just one year?"

"I feel better about a commitment of one year."

"How about if we amend this contract and give you an option to renew for another three years? This will give you time to see how good our relationship will be?"

Adam thought this over. "I suppose that'll work. I'm sure I'll know within the year if this is the future for me."

Ashley took Adam's original contract and placed it on the table next to its copy. She began making changes to them; the fly that was on one of the papers took flight.

Ashley initialed and signed the documents. When she was finished she gave them to Adam who did the same.

"Is that it?" He asked her.

"Stewart needs to enter his signature then it will be legal and binding. We'll have a contract that meets all the requirements of the law," Ashley informed him. She placed his paperwork back into its original folder.

"Dinar, I'm ready for you now."

Dinar's signing went quickly. He was satisfied with what he had seen. The loan was for twenty years. There was also a stipulation granting him a lifetime revolving credit line Now that they were done Ashley put everything in order. The folders were put back into her briefcase.

"That's it then. Stewart will sign your contracts. Each of you will receive your copy later today. I shall show you around our corporate headquarters now. We'll start with the directors' offices and go down from there," Ashley informed them.

The three of them stood up and began to leave. Adam glanced over at the hamsters' cage. Both hamsters were now spinning round and round within the cage's wheel.

After touring the building, viewing the other directors' offices, and observing their operations Ashley led Adam and Dinar to the dining room. It was on the high rise's sixth floor occupying the southwest corner. The room was as elegant as it was spacious. Eight crystal chandeliers hung from the ceiling. The floor beneath them was composed of beech wood. Of the four walls one was entirely mirrored, another partially held pictures and the remaining two were entirely of tinted glass. The dining tables were placed in such a way that a view of the outer world could readily be seen.

"Is this a private restaurant or is it available to the public?" Dinar asked Ashley.

"This is a special room Stewart and we directors use for entertaining our business clients and other guests. It's not a restaurant per se. Rather, it's a room for both dining and entertaining whatever the case may be."

"That explains the fancy wood flooring," Adam said.

"That's Stewart," Ashley responded. "The others will be here shortly, so, Adam, you and Dinar please take a seat next to the table's head," she requested and then left the room.

"I'm excited, aren't you?" Dinar claimed.

"It's been some day," Adam added.

"I wouldn't mind bonking that Ashley. She's a sexpot."

Adam laughed hard. "Is that all you can think about now?"

"It must be the money," Dinar figured rubbing his thumb on his gold watch.

"No, it's your overindulgent sense mind making you a victim of your habits. You know, Dinar, I think if they cut the top of your head off we'd find nothing but a bunch of pussies running around and around."

Dinar laughed at that remark.

Adam could clearly envision Dinar's mind's eye creating the scene he had just described to him. It would be six half women torsos going around in a circle, no head, no chest nor arms, just their bottom halves, nude from the waist down.

"I don't know where you come up with these things," Dinar spoke out then laughed some more.

"Glad you liked it. I'm going to look around the room while we wait."

Dinar got up with Adam. Together, they went over to the pictures on the wall. "I recognize this one, Dinar. It's a copy of the one Stewart has on his office wall. It's the eight company directors sitting at his conference table."

They moved closer to the photo. Each director had a label superimposed on or in front of him. Stewart's said 'President, VP and CEO,' Ashley Karmas, seated next to him, had affixed, 'Secretary, Treasurer, and Legal Director.' Going clockwise from there were Desiree Shaya, 'Lifetime Marketing Director,' Richard Eagleton, 'Recruitment Director,' Sam Skara, 'Revolving Investment Director,' Jaya Drake, 'Purchasing Director,' Ray Karnan, 'Accounting Director,' and finally Vicki Karnan, 'Customer Relations & Personnel Director.'

"Interesting photo," Adam said.

He and Dinar circled the room and then returned to their seats. In a short while Stewart and his crew entered the room.

"And here are our latest acquisitions," Stewart exclaimed. He walked over to them and clapped them on their backs. "I have you're your contracts here. It's official. Adam has treaded cautiously," he told the others. "But we've got these two young men under contract with Universal Holdings." He handed the two new recruits their papers.

"Way to go," Richard exclaimed. "Welcome to the crowd."

"Good move, Adam," Desiree claimed. "I'll enjoy working closer with you."

"Adam's office will be one floor from yours," Ashley told Desiree.

"Well, that's convenient."

"Yes, it is," Ashley agreed.

Adam noticed the cunning grin on Ashley's lips.

"Let us all sit now and we'll proceed with the meal," Stewart told them. He picked up a gold plated bell from the table and shook it.

Two waiters entered the room, went to the table and began taking each person's beverage and meal choices. There were four entrees to choose from, steak, shrimp, salmon, or turf & surf. Adam chose the salmon, Dinar the steak. The others went for the shrimp, steak or a combination of the two.

"Our new recruits received satisfying checks today," Stewart disclosed. "Are your plans still the same, Adam?"

"Yes, I'm buying my first house."

"And you, Dinar, will all your money go into your store?" Stewart asked him.

"I'm considering a gold ring or two," he answered. "The rest of the money will go towards my business," he added.

"Fine and good," Stewart declared.

"Where are you going to buy your new home?" Desiree asked Adam.

"I like the Camelback area."

"Good location," Richard claimed. "That'll put you close to us. Desiree and I live just above the base of the mountain."

"Stewart likes that," Desiree inserted. "He can watch us from above."

174

Ashley got a kick out of Desiree's statement. "The watchful eye of Stewart Demaya is ever upon us," she cried out. "But then Stewart's the one who's put us where we're at in the first place," she concluded.

"Yes, indeed," Jaya agreed.

The waiters brought out their drinks. Everyone talked about Universal Holdings and what the future held both for it and themselves. Sam and Jaya, Ray and Vicki, Richard and Desiree talked loudly about the company, its rapid growth and the affects it had on their lives. Stewart sat calmly listening to them. Every once in a while he and Ashley nodded contentedly to one another.

Once the beverages were consumed and salads nearly finished the waiters carried out the entrees. As Adam waited to be served, he let his mind drift. He thought about the big future waiting for him. He, and of course Taneka, would spend happy years together. They would enjoy the world and all its comforts through their love. What more could they ask for? Life had sweetness and he had fallen into it. Moonlight cruises, moonlight smooches, fine foods and all the pleasures they could ever hope for lay in wait for them. All he had to do was stay with the plan, Stewart's plan. He must be a dedicated 'team player.' He must play the game and help win the 'corporate profit.' He wasn't opposed to this. He understood the value of businesses; they had their places in the world. But he must never allow that world to consume him. He and Taneka were to have their life's' together. His place in worldly matters hadn't mattered much before. But where did he stand in all of this now? How would this new business contract affect him? Would he see things differently? Act differently?

His office was going to be located at the headquarters of Universal Holdings, the site of international workings, a massively expanding center of Stewart Demaya's world. Is this what he really wanted? Stewart was generous, he knew what others wanted. And then there's Ashley Karmas by his side. Demaya offered the world, she kept it running. She was like a solar recharging generator. He was the sun. He set the rules, she enforced them. He laid out a universal matrix, she regulated it. It was all legal. You play the game their way, here are its rules. You stay with us; we'll fulfill your desires. Poor Dinar, he's locked himself into a long term commitment. But, who knows, maybe it's what he needs? Why can't this be the case for you Adam Langston? Why are you so hung up about this new position? What can possibly go wrong in taking it?

The realtor stopped the car in front of Adam's apartment complex. Adam and Taneka stepped out and thanked the woman, a friend of Edwina's. Adam told the realtor he would call her the next day and then she drove off.

It was the end of the third day of house hunting. The daytime temperature had climbed once more into three digits and it would stay that way throughout the summer. They had gone from air conditioned car, out to the heat of the day, and then into an air conditioned home, back out to the heat of the day, a return into an air conditioned car and so on.

"Do you want anything to drink?" Adam asked Taneka.

His apartment was cool and comfortable.

"One of your lemon spritzers will do nicely," she told him.

He went into the kitchen and returned with two bottles. They went to his sofa.

"I like that Spanish house near Camelback best," he said handing the drink to her.

"It's older and more expensive than the others," she reminded him.

"I know, but you can't beat its location. It also has a large lot. I'm going to make an offer on it tomorrow. I'll put down a good amount that will keep the payments low. I can afford it now."

"It's your money. I just want you to be satisfied with what you choose."

"Will you live with me? We'll have a roomy house. There'll be lots of privacy on that acre of land."

"I'll think about it, Adam."

"You know I love you. I want you near me."

"Don't press your luck," she retorted.

"It's not luck that we found each other."

"That's not what I meant."

"We're meant to be together."

"Stop begging."

"I'm not begging."

"You may have found me but you can't have me," she said teasing him.

"Oh yes I can." He moved towards her. She ran into the bedroom. He followed her. "I've got you now," he cried out grabbing a hold of her.

"Now what are you going to do?"

"Did you take the pill?"

"Hundreds."

"No baby?"

"Not this time."

"How about a ravage and pillage?"

"Promises, promises."

"That was fun. Want to do it again?" Adam asked half seriously.

Taneka raised her head. "Don't press you luck."

"Now where have I heard those words before?" Adam said rolling over onto his side. His head was on the pillow next to hers.

"In joy I came, in joy I am, in joy I shall return once again."

"What's that you're singing, Tan?"

"I don't know. It's something I heard long ago.

"The joy of sex, Tan?"

"I don't think soooo," she said stretching out the word so. I don't think we go on to the next world when having sex, Adam."

"It would be pleasant."

"What? Five minutes of sexual joy cannot replace an infinite joy. First of all you'd need a physical body. Since we leave ours behind that leaves this notion out. Besides, the happiness I feel when I'm with you far surpasses the temporary pleasures of sex."

"My, doesn't that sound like Harish," Adam teased her.

"Actually, Adam, it's your sister's wise summation on this subject."

"Yeah, coached by Harish, and I don't mean to take anything away from either of them. Edwina's a bright girl and, as they say, an old soul."

178

"We're lucky to have her."

"Fortunate is a better word."

"Okay, fortunate to have her. What do you want for dinner?" She said changing the subject.

"More of you."

A month's waiting for the closing passed by, Adam signed the escrow papers in the morning. By noon, he was in his new house supervising the delivery of furniture. By mid-afternoon everything was in place and he returned to work.

Adam was quite comfortable in the spacious office he was given at Universal Holdings. Like his new home furniture, he furnished his office in oak. The new desk, chairs and working cabinets provided by Stewart were of solid oak not the commonly used compressed wood with oak laminates. His flooring was part oak wood and part beige carpet.

The office was one floor below Stewart and his main staff. Adam loved the view of The Valley below him and of Camelback Mountain in the distance. His house was not far from its base; however, from his present vantage point, it was too far away to be seen.

A new home, a new job, a new stage in Adam's life had begun. His responsibilities had increased from one fitness club to twelve. At least he wasn't directly involved with each club's daily activity. He no longer had direct contact with club members. That meant he didn't have to try and please everyone. He wouldn't miss that. Now he just had the twelve club managers to oversee and to keep motivated.

Adam looked at the desk clock. He picked up the phone, called Taneka, and reminded her to be at his house by seven. When they were finished talking Adam worked for the next hour putting in and retrieving out information on his computer. At three o'clock he took a break, left his office and rode the elevator down to the sixth floor. From there he went directly to the break room. The room was at the opposite end of the floor from the formal dining area where he and Dinar had dined the day they had signed their contracts.

Adam went to the vending machines. He dropped the required coins into both of the machines, removed his choices, and then found a seat at an empty corner table. Once settled, he broke open an oatmeal cookie's plastic wrapper, removed the cookie and bit into it.

"Hey, look who's here, our new boy wonder," Richard shouted out.

Adam glanced up from his cookie. Richard and Sam were standing next to him.

"How do you like it here?" Sam asked him.

"It's different."

"Hopefully different in a good way," Sam claimed.

"Yes, I'd say so. What are you two up to?" Adam asked.

"The same as you, we're here on break," Sam declared.

Sam sat down next to Adam. Richard headed for the vending machines. He returned with two cans of coke and gave one to Sam and then sat down beside him.

"Sam here is a happy man," Richard let out. "Tell Adam what you've done."

Sam's head went up. He leaned forward, smiled broadly showing his yellowing teeth then spoke. "I got Jaya another ring."

"You found a replacement then?" Adam said.

"This is not the same kind. I got her a wedding ring," he broadcast proudly again displaying his yellowing teeth.

"The poor sucker's going to get married," Richard cried out.

"Congratulations, when's the wedding, Sam?" Adam asked.

He shook his balding head. "She hasn't even seen the wedding ring yet."

"But, you are engaged aren't you."

"Sort of, Adam, sort of. That's one of the reasons I replaced Jaya's diamond. We've never discussed a wedding. That first ring just put us together."

"Now Sam's going to give Jaya the ring and they'll set a date," Richard inserted.

"I'm happy for both you and Jaya, Sam," Adam said and then took another bite into his oatmeal cookie. When he was done he tore off the tab on his protein bottle, took a big swig and mused over what Sam had just told him. He wondered how Taneka would react if he surprised her with a ring. That would involve a big commitment on his part. He was already facing two new ones now, a mortgage on a new house and a new job with greater responsibilities.

Adam lowered the hallway's thermostat to seventy-five. His guests would soon be arriving, first Edwina with Harish and then Taneka after that. He walked through the house inspecting each room. Everything was in order so he went out to the kitchen and set plates on his new oak dining table. They were going to have a simple meal. Taneka was bringing subs for them.

Adam switched on the television. He watched the news on CNN for fifteen minutes then the doorbell rang. He switched off the TV and answered the door.

Harish stepped in and shook Adam's hand. Edwina followed him on in. She kissed her brother on his cheek.

"We brought you a housewarming gift." Edwina handed him a package about twelve inches high and eight wide.

Adam led them into the kitchen. He found a knife and opened the package. "It's a Buddha," he exclaimed.

"You can put it in your meditation room once you've established one."

"What are you getting at, Harish?"

"Your new life, my friend. It will happen, this I foretell."

Adam eyed his sister. "What's this, has he become a fortuneteller?"

"Not a fortuneteller but one who helps mend fortunes," Harish answered for her.

"I see," Adam said.

"Do you?" Harish fired back.

"Okay, enough," Adam spoke out laughing out loud.

"Take us on a tour, Brother," Edwina ordered.

Adam led them through the house.

"Good job, Adam," Edwina said after they were done. "The furnishings look great."

"Taneka helped pick them out."

"You two did well," Harish told him. "How's the new job coming along?"

"It's going well. However, it's more detailed than my last one. Everything is at a different level. How about you? Have you come to a decision yet?"

"I'm going to let Dinar buy me out."

"Really? What will you do without the store?"

Harish looked over at Edwina. "Adam, your sister and I are going overseas. I've negotiated a good price from my cousin. I won't have to work for a long while if I wish. I'm taking Edwina to see some of the world's sacred sites. We'll finish up in India."

"Wow that sounds exciting. Edwina, what are you doing about your job?"

"It's been taken care of. They're giving me a sabbatical so to speak."

"What prompted this travel, Harish?"

"It's actually been in the back of mind for some time. I haven't had a real vacation the past two years. Now I'll have freedom from the store and the money for travel," he told them." Harish laughed. "It's a great feeling. You ought to try it sometime."

"Very funny, don't rub it in," Adam responded. "Although, who knows what the next year will bring?" He added.

"I think Taneka has arrived," Edwina told him. She walked over to the front door and opened it.

Taneka entered the foyer holding a large white bag. On its side ,in red lettering, were the words 'Subs Galore.'

"Let me help you with that," Edwina said.

Adam hugged Taneka, they kissed and then everyone went on into the kitchen.

During the meal the two couples excitedly talked about the changes in their lives and the changes they felt would come. The mysteries of the world were opening and they were a part of them.

It was well into the evening when Harish and Edwina decided it was time to leave.

"It was a pleasant night, Adam. Enjoy your new home," Harish told him.

"Thanks for having us," Edwina added. "See you tomorrow, Tan."

Taneka and Adam watched them drive off.

"They make a great pair," Taneka claimed.

"They deserve each other. They're good people."

"The trip they're planning sounds wonderful. I'm going to miss them."

"We both are, Tan."

"I've got something for you?"

"What do you mean?"

"It's a housewarming gift. Stay here, I'll be right back," she told him and then went off down the hallway.

When she returned she was wearing only a bath towel held together by a red ribbon.

"What's this?"

"It's your present. Come over here and unwrap it."

Summer advanced to August. Harish's sale of his half of the business was completed. Dinar moved ahead with his plans of opening a chain of Far East Imports. Soon he would have half a dozen stores spread throughout the Valley. Stewart helped him with their staffing. Together they handpicked six managers. Everything was looking up for Harish's cousin. Stewart and he were quite pleased with their relationship.

With the sale of his business interest, Harish was freed from responsibilities and monetary issues. Now that he had the time and the necessary funds for extensive travel he and Edwina put the final touches on their overseas' travel. They would leave the Valley in early September and fly to Europe. Their first destination was London. After that it was will-of- the- whim. Their trip had a planned beginning and planned ending. In between would be a go-with-the-flow. However, England was definitely the beginning and India was the ending. Five or six months or so of sightseeing meant they wouldn't set their eyes again on Phoenix until the spring.

Adam was firmly established in his home and new job. Once he had everything in order, overseeing twelve health clubs became easier. It was happy with his new position and what if offered him. He always enjoyed trying out new exercise equipment and now he had ample opportunity to do just that. He, Taneka, Harish and Edwina flew to a trade show in Reno in September. Adam was in seventh heaven. He met various equipment manufacturers, trained on their new machines and talked fitness. On top of that he was able to purchase whatever he liked for the Universal Fitness clubs.

After the trade convention ended Adam and Taneka had an afternoon to their selves. They decided to see old Reno. As they made their way along the streets they stopped from time to time peering into the store windows. When they came to a jewelry store Adam took a hold of Taneka's hand.

"Do you see those rings in there?" He asked pointing his free hand at the window in front of them.

"Up there? It's a nice display. What about the rings?"

"I'm buying you one. You get to pick it out."

"What do you mean, Adam?"

"We're getting married."

"Hold on there, Adam Langston. Are you asking me to marry you?"

"You might say that."

"And just when is this wedding supposed to take place? Certainly not here in Reno."

"Tan, don't get flustered. I'm, that is we, are getting engaged."

"And you're making the decision and announcement for both us now, is that it?"

"Yep. It's time."

"You're being compulsive."

"Well," Adam said squeamishly, 'I guess you're right." Then he added defensively, "I don't do it in everything you know."

"That's true."

"So, how about this time, Tan? Come on let's go in."

"And this is the way you plan to do it?"

Adam got down on one knee. "Taneka, will you marry me?"

She blushed. "Do you mean this, Adam?"

"I do."

"That's what said in front of a minister."

"I know. So what do you say, Tan?"

186

"I do."

They both laughed hard and went into the store. She found a ring she liked. He bought it. They came out all smiles. They walked hand in hand down the street speaking love and unconditional loyalty to one another. Adam asked her to move in with him. Taneka told him she wasn't ready for that, she was old fashioned. They'd live together only when they were married. She wanted a June wedding. Adam agreed.

Later they caught up with their friends at their hotel. Taneka broke the news to them by showing off her engagement ring.

"You've actually done it, Adam. You're going to take the plunge."

"That's right, Edwina, I'm jumping right into the matrimonial pool," he said with a huge smile on his face.

"When's the wedding going to be?" Harish wished to know.

"Next June," Taneka told him.

"That's great," Edwina declared. "Harish and I will be back in time to help you with any arrangements you might need."

"Why don't we all go for a hike around Lake Tahoe tomorrow?" Adam asked everyone. "We've got the day free."

"It sounds good to me," Edwina said. "What about you, Harish?"

"Yes, it will give us one last outing together before we leave the country."

The next day they shopped for a picnic lunch. Along the way to Lake Tahoe they stopped at a sporting goods store and purchased two day packs. Then they drove on to a trailhead next to the lake and Adam parked his rental car by it. The men organized their new packs. Everyone was in good spirits. They dressed lightly, wearing T-shirts and shorts. The weather was mild compared to the Arizona heat they had left three days earlier. There were isolated scattered clouds in a blue sky. Birds were actively flying in the air and amongst the lake's surrounding trees.

The hike was easy, the ground was fairly level. After a while they came to two large rocks located in the water next to the shoreline. The two couples sat opposite one another, each perched on a separate rock with their feet dangling over the water below them. Adam and Harish opened their packs, removed water bottles and dispersed them.

"Look at that eagle up there," Taneka said pointing to the sky above the lake. "I think it has a fish in its claws."

"That's not an eagle, Tan. It's an osprey," Adam told her.

"They are similar in appearance to an eagle," Harish claimed, "but they're not the real birds of freedom. They're very good fishermen, and few prey are able to escape those imprisoning talons."

"A nest must be nearby," Edwina reasoned. "The trees, mountains and the lake make for a beautiful and peaceful setting here," she added.

"Life's simple things give the most pleasure," Harish claimed. "Nature, the love of it, and the love of others, this is what we're meant to enjoy. What sayest thou, Adam?"

"I sayest thou art right. Why else would we be on this planet?"

"To learn our lessons and to change ourselves," Harish answered.

"Adam has changed. Falling in love has done that to him," Edwina claimed.

"We all have to learn to love," Harish responded. "We have to find balance. Until we find it our lessons are not complete."

"You're saying life's a school and we are its students," Taneka conjectured.

"That's right," Harish answered. "And it all began when God put the first race of people on the planet."

"The first race of people?" Adam asked wondering about Harish's choice of words. "What about Adam and Eve?"

"They're one and the same. Yogananda explained it in *Autobiography of a Yogi*."

"Is this the same Yogananda who established the gardens in Encinitas?" Taneka wanted to know.

"Yes. I like to quote from his work. He came to this county in 1920. His mission was to unite the East and the West by showing the similarity of Christ's and Krishna's teachings. Whenever I speak of spiritual matters I only discuss what I've experienced or come to know via self-realized Masters."

"What do you mean by that?" Taneka asked.

"A self-realized person is one who has perfected himself and knows God. He has direct experience of God. He doesn't parrot the scriptures, nor does he explain the nature of things through church dogma. He uses the intuitive perception developed in his meditations and the helping hand of God to discern truth."

"Tell us the Adam and Eve story," Taneka requested.

Harish drank the last of his spring water, cleared his throat and then began the explanation. "The story is similar to one found in the

189

Hindu scriptures. Adam and Eve were symbolic of the first race of men. The race was put here in order to enjoy the wonders of the world and then to move on to God's other mansions. They had the ability to create children by thought and births were accomplished by what we now call Immaculate Conception. And here's the catch. God warned them not to indulge in sex. Watch and study the mineral, plant, and animal world but don't engross yourself in it. If you get caught up in the physical reproductive act you will lose your divinity and your abilities because you will be subjected to the laws that are needed to hold the physical world together.

"What about the apple, the garden of Eden and the rest?" Taneka inquired.

"Adam and Eve, the first race, were overcome by their desire to experience the animals' reproductive act. This is the Fall of Man. They experienced sex physically and they fell from their divine state. This led to other desires and to worry, weakness, jealousy, boredom, and the clutches of karma.

"The Adam and Eve Story is symbolic. The Tree of Life is man's treelike nervous system. Humans are upturned trees. Our hair and cranial nerves are the roots, our spinal cord, the trunk, and our nerves, the branches. The serpent is the life energy in the spine and the Garden is the human body. The Apple or Fruit is sensation. To eat of the Apple located in the midst of the Garden is to partake of the Forbidden Fruit of sexual intercourse. By doing so man's divine consciousness is lost."

"Just how is he lost," Adam asked.

"He's lost because he is now subjected to physical laws. Remember, he has become body conscious due to his unnecessary physical actions. As I said this leads to other desires, which, in turn, lead him to the law of karma. Every action returns to the actor."

"How are we supposed to overcome this, Harish?" Taneka wanted to know.

"Man lacks Divine Love. You see, our purpose in life is to each day battle our way back to the Divine. We are here to learn our lessons, work out our karma and end our desires. We have been given free will as a birthright. Now we must use it to destroy our ego, the pseudo-soul that makes us believe this physical world is all that is real and worthy."

"It all makes sense," Adam concluded. "But then," he added looking over at Taneka, "If we are to overcome this world and all desires we'll have to give up sex."

Harish laughed loudly. "You look so worried, my friend. Put your mind at ease. Nature has made the sex impulse very strong so that Creation might go on. Sex has its place in a marriage. But sex itself is not love. Sex and love are as far apart as the moon and the sun. In time, sex will fall away on its own accord. When it does it will have ceased to have mattered. Once we've experienced a higher and more blissful state, the limited short term joy of sex will seem as if nothing. And, when we discover that sex is just another desire keeping us from higher divine states, we will work harder at overcoming it. Remember what yoga does for us. It teaches us to look at ourselves honestly in the eye and find out what we are. Then, with all the strength of our soul, we try destroying the evil in us. The evil is anything that keeps or obstructs us from God-realization. I think if we would just fill ourselves with noble ideas, enjoy good music, pictures, good food, flowers and nature we would live in paradise."

"It all sounds wonderful yet difficult," Taneka confessed. "It's like we exist within a balancing act. We have to live in the world but not be of the world."

"Right now I'm trying to balance my hunger and need for food," Adam burst out.

"Harish has just given us food for the soul, Little Brother," Edwina teased.

"Adam's just had a filling of food for thought. Now he needs fuel for his tummy," Taneka cried out joining in the fun.

Chapter 9

Fall

Behind every rosebush of pleasure there is a rattlesnake of disillusionment. P. Yogananda

"How are things coming along with Richard?" Stewart was at his office desk; Ashley was sitting across from him.

"Richard won't be a problem, his egoistic desires make him easy prey for us," she responded. The effects of the role Demaya had given Ashley filled her with satisfaction; her face was glowing.

"Good, man's ego is our ally, without it you and I would have no place in this world," Demaya told her, his dark face leaking the evil he had within him.

"What's your plan now," she asked wanting more of what he offered.

"We must keep using Richard to get to Desiree, who, will in turn, get to Adam. I will continue filling her mind with thoughts of him. As to our other directors, we will use of them as needed."

"Your ways are so subtle. They haven't the faintest clue of your abilities," Ashley revealed. "You play so well upon their imperfections."

"They dance like marionettes to my tune, my dear."

"Especially Desiree," Ashley spoke out gleefully. "She's well named and a most useful tool."

"As long as there is desire there is no end to our hold on those who crave its fulfillment," Demaya proclaimed.

"Why do you put so much value on Adam?"

"We must not let that young man slip away. He has within him certain abilities that we will use. He is naïve, and with Harish now gone, easy to manipulate. We will tap into his hidden talents; this will draw more souls into the fold. If we lose him, his talents will work against us."

"What about Harish?"

"He's become harder to reach," Demaya answered with concern. "I still have to find a way to get to him. He, and those like him, threaten our existence."

"You did a clever thing having Dinar buy him out and getting him out of the country."

"And we shall make the most out of that," Demaya claimed.

The board of director's meeting was due to meet in ten minutes. Desiree wanted to go over a few things with Richard before then. She knocked lightly at his office door, and then hurriedly stepped into the room. Richard was seated at his desk. Ashley was behind him; her arms were wrapped around his shoulders."

"What's going on?" Desiree demanded.

"Nothing, we're just going over our reports for the meeting," Ashley told her.

Desiree's eyes narrowed and became snake-like. "Yeah, I'm sure that's all it is," she said sarcastically stomping out of the room.

Richard shrugged his shoulders. "Don't worry, she'll get over it."

"I'm not worried," Ashley claimed and then took her hands and caressed his blond locks.

Stewarts's office door opened slowly and Richard and Ashley entered the room. Desiree glared at the two of them. Richard gave her a quick, furtive glance and then he and Ashley went over to the conference table and took their places there.

"Good, we're all here now," Stewart announced. "I see everyone has their quarterly reports." As he spoke to them, his magnetic face and dark eyes shined upon them as if they had a light all of their own. "This past quarter," he went on, "has seen a spurt in the ongoing growth of Universal Holdings. For this I am quite pleased. Now I'd like to hear from each of you."

Ashley reported first. She said sales were up eight percent compared to the same quarter last year. Stewart beamed. He was happiest when Universal Holdings grew in number. As the world's population grew so did his business and his hold on it.

"Thank you, Ashley; I'm sure we are all happy to hear that. It's called job security; the larger the number, the larger the paycheck.

Ashley, I'll study your report in detail later," Stewart told her. "Now, let's hear from the rest of you."

The remaining six board members reported in the order of their seating.

"Splendid!" Stewart exclaimed after he heard the last one. "I'll read your reports fully this afternoon. Let's all keep working hard for the expansion of Universal Holdings.

"Now I'll speak of the four day cruise that I've planned for us. We shall set sail from San Diego on the best ship in my Norwegian fleet. Its elegance is second to none. Remember, our job is to both maintain and increase Universal Holdings. As such, we must see that our invited guests stay focused on our business while having a good time. As, per usual, I shall work my illusionary magic. With that said, we shall now indulge ourselves in the exquisite lunch prepared especially for you."

Stewart led them out of the room and down the hall like a pied piper. Desiree hesitated, stood back and waited. As soon as Ashley reached the doorway, Desiree hurriedly brushed into and past her; Ashley stumbled, threw her hands out and braced herself against the door's framework.

"Bitch!" Desiree yelled at her. She then left the room and joined the line of people who were following Demaya.

Taneka,

In the now passed summer days I have gathered the nectar blossoms of the sweet qualities growing in the garden of your soul.

Adam sent the message, wondered about Taneka's reply, and then went back to work on Universal Fitness's new membership contract. There were questions he had for Ashley concerning the changes she had made from the original form. He left his room and took the stairs leading up to the next floor. It was a short walk from there to her office. He found the door partially open so he walked in. He should have knocked. Ashley and Richard were behind the desk embracing and kissing one another. Adam backed out silently. Ashley's sultry eyes calmly watched him leave the room.

He walked down the hall. What he had just witnessed was no surprise to him. After all, Richard had told him that he was a victim of his habits. Adam shook this off. Those people, he thought, have their own rules. What they did was none of his business.

"Hey, Adam, come and join us," Ray Karnan called out to him. They were in the break room.

Adam bought a bottle of spring water from the dispensing machine and then joined Ray and Sam at the table. Sam reeked of smoke. Adam sat at the other side of the table from him.

"What's happening?" Sam asked.

Adam thought about the lover's embrace he had viewed only minutes ago. "Oh, not much," he replied.

"Ray was just showing me pictures of his new sports car," Sam announced.

Ray slid a photo in front of Adam.

"That's a sixty-two Corvette," Adam declared.

"I've wanted one for years," Ray told him.

"It's the sixth car in his collection," Sam stated.

"I wouldn't mind having something like that," Adam acknowledged.

"Then why don't you get one? You're making enough money now," Ray claimed.

Adam took out a protein bar from his pants pocket, removed the wrapper, and bit into the bar. "We'll see," he said.

"What's the good of money if you don't spend it on what you want?"

"Rays' right," Sam said. "You should get what you want. You work hard for it."

Ray began telling his companions about the other cars he was going to buy. Soon all of them were rattling on about their car fantasies.

Adam absently finished off his protein bar and spring water. "Guys, it's been interesting," he told them, "But I have to go now, I've got some work to wrap up. I've enjoyed our talk," he added, then stood up, threw his waste in the trash, and left the two men to their dreams.

After the waitress was gone, Taneka handed Adam a note. They were in a Mexican restaurant in Tempe. Adam unfolded the paper.

I find in your heart an ever increasing love divine. My human heart shall quench its thirst drinking from that love.

Adam folded up Taneka's note and slipped it into his pocket. He put his face to hers and kissed her soft, slender lips.

"What movie have you picked out for us tonight?" She asked when they were done.

"That's what you thought of my kiss?" He said in jest.

"Actually, I thought romance. Tell me we're going to a romantic love story."

Adam looked unsettled. "Well, I've picked out an action flick. There aren't any romances playing nearby."

"I see," Taneka said. "It's the male thing."

"You don't mind a flick with good action and storyline."

"Only if it's not violent and blood laden. I hope this will be the case tonight."

"I think it'll be entertaining."

"I hope so. How's everything going at work?"

Adam pictured the little incident in Richard's office. Deciding not to mention it he said, "I was on break with Ray and Sam. Ray just bought his sixth classic sports car."

"Why does he have so many?"

"He likes collecting them. It must be in his nature," Adam reasoned.

"Is Stewart all right with us not going on the cruise?"

"He didn't say anything one way or another when I told him. Stewart's happy, his business is thriving. It keeps him active. So why should our not going matter to him?"

The waitress arrived with their meals. They ate in silence for a while and then Adam spoke out.

"Tan, since I was a kid I've always wanted a Corvette or similar sports car. I'm thinking about getting one now."

"You already have a nice car. Why do you need another one?"

"Just for the fun of it. We can put the car's top down and cruise under the stars."

"Are you trying to convince me by making it seem romantic?"

"Tan, I'm just thinking of the fun."

"The question doesn't concern fun, Mr. Thomas Adam Langston. It's a question about necessities. Is the sports car a necessity or an unnecessary necessity?"

"Tan, Harish said it's all right to have some things, just don't get attached to them."

"He also said that if it's something we *have to have* then the need for it is wrong because we're already attached to it. It's simply an unnecessary necessity. So what's it for you?"

"It's a fulfillment of a desire. I don't have to have it but I would like to."

"Be careful, Adam."

"What do you mean?"

"Since you've moved into your new office and job you've become restless. Maybe you co-workers are creating the wrong environment for you."

"You're thinking that environment is stronger than willpower. Don't worry, Tan, I won't fall into that trap."

"Adam, I meant what I said in that note I just gave you. Our love is growing. My only concern is for your welfare. I want what's best for you."

"What's best for both of us," Adam added, then, anxious about the time, glanced at his cell phone. "We better eat quickly if we're going to make the movie."

Three hours later they left the movie theater.

"That was not one of the better films for us to have seen, Adam." They were in Adam's car on the way to Taneka's apartment.

"What do you mean? It wasn't ultra-violent. It had a decent storyline."

"It was those sex scenes. I don't need the detail."

"We have sex."

"Ours is in the privacy of our bedroom."

"I understand."

"Those scenes were too blatant. They pull our minds down. We have each other and that's enough. I think true love is purity. If our love is to grow into divine love we must keep sex in its proper place."

"It will have to be if it stands in our goal's way," he admitted.

"Your sister gave me two books before she and Harish left for Europe. One's about Ammachi, the hugging saint. She travels the world giving darshan, a spiritual blessing. She hugs everyone who comes to her. Her message is love and selfless service. The other book Edwina gave me is titled *Answers*. It contains the answers to questions Mother Meera, another saint, was asked. She gives darshan also. Unlike Ammachi, her darshan is done in complete silence. She is considered to be the Mother of Wisdom, Ammachi is the Mother of Love. There's information about them on the internet."

"Maybe someday we'll get to see them."

"I'd like that. Edwina told me about a third Mother, the Mother of World Peace. She was born into an affluent Western family. Her spiritual name is Loka Shanti Shakti."

"This is a start, Tan; if we decide it's the direction we want to go."

Adam finished rereading *A Separate Reality*. He had first read the book while in college. He had been intrigued by its subject matter, and, as a result, had ended up reading the author's other works. The writings were about white sorcery and the quest for knowledge. The author, Carlos Castaneda, claimed he was an apprentice of a Yaqui Indian sorcerer named Don Juan. Castaneda was deceased now.

Adam wondered if there was any information about him on the internet. He set the book down on his desk, went onto the internet and in a short time located a site and began reading what it had to say. To his dismay he discovered Castaneda's works were all a hoax. He had heard this once before but had never believed it. However, what he was reading now seemed to be final proof of the hoax. Castaneda's lifestyle was not that of a spiritual warrior. The man had fallen. He had started a sort of cult. The women who joined him were seduced by his charm and claim of sorcery powers. Some of them claimed that they had to have sex with him. This was part of the teachings he was offering them. Ultimately, Castaneda died of cancer. After his death three women disappeared, one's remains were found near her abandoned car in Death Valley, the other two women have never been heard from. The fact that Castaneda did not follow and practice the path he wrote about disturbed Adam. He realized that the critics were right about their assessment of Castaneda—he was a fraud. It's a shame, he thought. The author's books were well-written, fictional novels, and on their own would have done well. Why then did Carlos Castaneda live the big lie? People were led to believe his writings were factual. They believed Castaneda was a spiritual warrior seeking knowledge and what he had experienced was real. Instead, he was a disillusioned millionaire caught in the delusionary web of the world.

Adam backed out of the site and turned off the computer.

"Hey buddy, how's it going?"

It was Dinar and his usual way of entering Adam's office.

"I haven't seen you two for a while," Adam said. Melia was with Dinar.

"We've been busy with the new stores and the cruise," Dinar told him.

"Congratulations on your job promotion, Adam. You're a bright boy. I knew you'd work your way up in the company," Melia said flattering him.

"What brings you two by today?"

"Dinar had a meeting with Stewart. I tagged along," Melia answered.

"How was the cruise?"

"You should've been there. Stewart worked his usual magic. The food and partying couldn't have been better," Dinar spoke out.

"There was an incident though," Melia claimed.

"What kind of incident?" Adam asked.

"It seems Rich and Ashley have a thing going. Desiree must've seen something. They all were in the lounge together. Desiree tossed her drink on Ashley, and then there was a shoving match. Rich had to break it up. He finally got them settled down and Ashley left."

"Does Stewart know about this?"

"I think so," Dinar answered. "But these things don't bother him. He's only interested in sailing his business ship."

"But this must rock his boat," Adam said in jest."

"Hey, as long as things get done and we get what we want what does it matter?"

"Dinar's right, what does it matter? It just adds a little spice to this world."

"Melia, sometimes too much spice ruins the meal," Adam retorted.

Twenty minutes after Dinar and Melia left, Adam felt a strong urge to get on his computer. The image of sports cars kept playing before his mind's eye. He typed in *Craigslist*, looked and waited. To his surprise an image of Stewart Demaya appeared on the screen. He gaped at it, as he did so a voice from behind spoke out startling him.

"What are you doing?" The voice said.

"Stewart, I didn't expect to find you here," Adam said. He was feeling trepidation and did not know why.

"What are you looking for on *Craigslist*?" Stewart asked, pretending he had no idea what it was.

"Well, I . . . just suddenly felt a strange and sudden impulse to look for a sports car," Adam revealed.

"That's fine. You can become a collector like Ray," Stewart told him.

"I don't know, maybe. Ray already has six of them."

"Adam, you can have whatever your heart desires. Believe that and believe in me.

A week later, Adam went out and bought his sports car. It was a green Cobra, a replica of Ford's model. An original factory Cobra would have cost too much. As it was, the car took most of his savings. Taneka was not pleased with his purchase. She told him he had acted impulsively. Eventually, however, she came around and accepted the car. The two of them made a day trip to Sedona and Oak Creek Canyon in the topless Cobra. That outing had been fun. The weather that day was comfortably warm. The open air had blown through their hair and made them feel free.

At five O'clock Adam locked his office door and went to Stewart's office.

"Adam, take a seat. I liked your quarterly report. It appears the club managers are learning well from you. The new fitness clubs definitely are going to provide a big boost for this company. You keep up the good work and we'll be expanding again in marketplace next year."

"I'll do my best."

"Richard was out on promotions today. I have a package I'd like you to give him. Since you now live so close to him you can drop it off for me."

"No problem. I'll be at our Scottsdale club at the end of the day. After that I can deliver the package for you."

Stewart handed him a box about ten by twelve inches in size. Adam turned to leave.

"Wait, I have something else for you," he said. He opened his desk drawer and removed an envelope. "Here, these Cardinals' passes are for you, your gal, Richard, and Desiree. They'll get you into my private box at the stadium."

"Thanks, Stewart. What do you think of your team's playoff chances?"

"That's a tough call. We lost a five time all-pro player when Johnny Ortiz died. That hurt our offense," he claimed. "It's a good thing we have a strong defense," he added reassuringly. "Enjoy the game."

After Adam left Ashley visited with Demaya. "Have you moved forward with your plans?" She asked him.

"It has all been arranged. Adam will drop by Desiree's house, later this afternoon.

"Then you've talked to her about it."

"I have done that in my subtle ways."

"Ah, then you've given her mental suggestions."

"As is my way. She believes what's going to happen today will give her satisfaction, and it will be something she deserves. She also sees it as a way of getting even with Richard."

"You know how to stir the pot," Ashley said contentedly.

Demaya grinned devilishly, satisfied that once again he was going to get his way

Adam drove his green Cobra into Richard and Desiree's circular drive. He parked there, stepped out of the car with Stewart's package tucked under his arm, and walked to the home's front entrance where he rang the doorbell. He waited, nobody came. He rang again. This time the bell was answered and the door opened. Desiree, wearing a miniscule, hot pink bikini stood in the doorway.

"Hi, Adam, is that for me?" She asked looking at the package he was holding.

"Stewart asked me to give this to Richard."

"Please come in."

Adam walked into the front room. Desiree followed him eyeing him all over. "Have you been to the gym?"

"Yes, how do you know that?"

"By the gym shorts and shirt you're wearing," she answered staring at him with her penetrating eyes.

"Of, course, my clothes," he muttered out loud.

"Come take a seat on the sofa," she requested.

He sat down. She sat next to him. "Where's Richard?" He asked.

"He went with Sam to buy some sporting gear. We're all going deer hunting up north next weekend. It's the beginning of bow hunting season you know."

"No, I didn't know that."

"It doesn't matter," she said smiling strangely at him.

Adam felt nervous and uncomfortable. He pulled out the tickets Stewart had given him. "Stewart wants the four of us to go to the Cardinals' game Sunday."

"If that's what Stewart wants then we better go."

Adam put the tickets back in his pocket. He set Richard's package down next to a bowl of fruit on the table in front of him.

"Please give this to Richard. I'm going to head home now."

"What's your hurry? Are you hungry?" She asked. "Take some of this fruit to satisfy your appetite," she insisted pointing to fruit bowl.

"Well, I don't know," he told her. His anxiety increased and he stood up.

She stood up with him.

"Here," she said. She reached into the bowl, came out with an apple and handed it to him. "Go ahead it's good for you."

Adam accepted the fruit. Delusion's desire dangled dangerously around them. He bit into the apple. She dropped the top of her suit. He looked incredulously at her. Two perfect 38's, cocked and ready for action were pointed straight at him.

He choked. She pressed herself against him. He gasped for breath. She wrapped snake-like around him and squeezed him tightly. The apple in his throat loosened.

Desiree stepped back. Adam stared again at those perfect 38's. Suddenly, she pulled his shorts down.

"Oh God," he voiced weakly.

Desiree stood up before him. She kicked off her bottoms then pulled Adam's shirt off him. He was in a daze. She grabbed him and they fell together onto the couch. * * *

208

"You were good," Desiree told him after they had quenched the day's desire. Then she pushed him aside. Her eyes were glassed over and looking elsewhere.

Adam saw the vacant look. "I don't know how this happened," he said.

"We wanted each other," she responded. "We wanted it, all of it."

"It was lust," Adam said feeling the beginning of remorse.

"It was wonderful animalistic sex," Desiree claimed.

"But what about the others?" He asked her.

"What others?"

"Richard and Taneka."

Desiree held up her hand. "Do you see a ring?" She cried out.

Adam thought about the one on Taneka's hand.

"What does it matter, we're not married to them?" She argued.

"What are we going to do now?

"We get dressed and you go home."

"What about the game on Sunday. We'll all be together."

"We go to the game. That's what Stewart wants."

They got dressed. Desiree walked him to his car.

"Thanks for the package, Adam."

"That was for Richard."

"I'm, referring to the package you gave me," Desiree declared. The glow in her green eyes had returned. They were magnetic and inviting. She blew him a kiss, turned, and went back to the house she shared with Richard.

Adam drove off, baffled by it all. Everything had happened so fast. Sure he wanted Desiree, what man wouldn't? But hadn't his sexual desires for other women ended when he met Taneka?

He began questioning everything. What did he want in life? What did he need from it? Memories came to him of a girl he had once slandered when in high school. His friends, and schoolmates, wanted to know about any sex play they may have had on their date. His ego was being tested, so he boasted and lied. He told them that he had gone to third base with the girl. Word got back to her. He had defamed her. Why? It was done just because he wanted to stand tall in front of those boys. He was young, dumb and a teenager. He wished he could find that girl, now a grown woman, and apologize for his ignorant act.

His past had just replayed itself. Maybe it was a little different this time, but it would have the same effect. He had given his loyalty to Taneka. She trusted him. Now he was hurting her.

Adam pulled into his garage and shut off the Cobra. He went into the house, dropped his keys on the kitchen counter and then hurried to the master bathroom. Removing his clothing, he stepped into the shower and cleansed himself. Then he grabbed a towel, dried himself off, and went into his study. He turned on the laptop. There were three emails. He opened the one from Taneka.

I am thy tiny hummingbird dipping my beak into our hearts' love. I sip the nectar of our united souls.

Disgusted with himself, Adam shut down the computer and went off to bed. His sleep was short and restless. * * *

On the appointed Sunday, Adam and Taneka drove over to Richard and Desiree's house. From there, the two couples went in Richard's car to the Cardinals' game. This is what Stewart Demaya wanted, the four of them together, whatever his reason may be. Adam barely spoke a word on the way to the game; he was too busy with his thoughts. He worried that he was becoming like Demaya's others— just another pawn on his chess board.

Richard pulled into the special parking lot next to the stadium. The four of them got out of the car. Richard was spotted by the nearby crowd. Soon there were autograph seekers surrounding him. Adam and the women waited patiently for him. Richard was in his element. He signed the last of their papers and then hurriedly left with his friends. They went together to Stewart's private box. Desiree asked Adam to sit next to her. He tactically refused. The two women ended up sitting next to each other, the men, on either side of them.

Taneka was aware of Adam's strange behavior. Tension filled the air. Whenever Desiree spoke to Adam he answered her briefly without looking at her. He seemed nervous and not at all himself. Richard was unusually quiet. He spoke only about the play that was taking place on the field below them.

As soon as the football game ended the two couples left the stadium and drove back to Richard and Desiree's house. Adam and Taneka did not stay long. They thanked the couple for the day and then left in Adam's car.

"What's going on?" Taneka asked as soon as they drove off.

"What do you mean?"

"There's something funny about you as well as Richard and Desiree."

211

"Desiree's just mad at him. Rich is having an affair with Ashley," he blurted out.

"Oh, I see. That's not good. But I'm feeling there's something more to this."

"What else could there be?" Adam answered. He felt like crawling within himself.

"I'm sorry to hear about them. However, my woman's intuition is telling me you're hiding something. I feel this and I feel your sadness."

Adam swallowed the lump in his throat. "I'll tell you when we get to the house."

Six long minutes later Adam pulled his car into his drive. He pushed the remote's button on the car's visor. The garage door opened. He drove in and parked next to the green Cobra.

"Can I get you anything?" He asked her when they reached the kitchen.

"No," she answered taking a seat at the counter. "Tell me what's going on."

He sat down next to her. "I don't know how it happened."

"How what happened?"

"The thing with Desiree."

"You mean Richard's affair?"

"No, that's not it," he said and then went on and confessed what had transpired with Desiree.

Taneka was in shock, her eyes moistened. "I can't believe you did this, Adam," Taneka said Tears began rolling down her cheeks. "You broke our trust and commitment."

"I couldn't help it. She seduced me," he claimed in his defense.

"That's not a valid excuse!" She shouted. "You could've stopped it. How do you expect to have a marriage if there's no loyalty?"

"I'm so sorry, Tan. Please forgive me. I love you. It was stupid of me."

Taneka pulled off the ring from her finger and tossed it on the counter. It landed on its edge, rolled twice around itself, and then came to a rest on its side.

"Please don't do that," Adam pleaded. "Please put it back on."

"The ring spun twice, that's exactly how many chances I'm giving you. You've used up one, that leaves you with one," she reported.

"I don't understand."

"I'm giving you a second chance to make things work. I'm doing this in hopes your love for me is strong enough to overcome your weakness. You have to prove that your love is real."

"But we are soulmates."

"We are? That has to yet be proven."

"Then you're still going to see me?"

"I'm giving you a second chance to get your act together, Take me home now."

"Then what?"

'You've hurt me deeply. We need time to see where our relationship is going. I'll let you know if, and when, I'm ready to resume it. Just take me home. Then don't visit, email or phone me. I'll contact you if I'm ready. Got it?" * * *

"I'm not going hunting with you today, Jaya told them.

She was standing in the motel's parking lot. It was the latter part of October.

"Why not?" Desiree asked her.

"I don't want to shoot Bambi's mother."

Desiree laughed. "It's just a deer, Jaya. It's not like we lack them."

"I don't care. You go. I'm putting on my makeup and warmer clothing. I have to look at property with a realtor and today's a good day for it. Then I'm shopping Flagstaff. Besides, I'm not a hunter like you. It's dangerous out there. You don't know what might happen. Everyone's camouflaged and shooting at anything that moves."

"Jaya's looking at cabins for us," Sam said in her defense.

"Let's get going then," Richard commanded.

Richard drove north out of town. The San Francisco Mountains were on his left; Mount Humphreys stood out amongst them. They came to a red dirt road and turned left onto it. Five miles up the road two SUVs were sitting in a pullout.

"We aren't the only ones here," Sam claimed.

They drove on another two miles and passed a parked truck along the way. Richard found an area he liked and pulled the car to the side of the road. He turned off the engine. They were in the lower foothills. The woods around them were showing autumn's colors.

"This is as good a place as any to start the hunt," Richard reported.

The three of them gathered their individual gear, a day pack, a bow, and a quiver filled with arrows. They walked into the woods,

Richard leading the way. In a short time they reached a small valley. They stepped into it. The sky was clear; the sun's rays found and warmed them.

"We need to spread out now," Richard told them. "I'll go to the left. We must stay within the cover of the trees and be within shouting range. We'll use our whistle to call out if we need to locate each other. Remember, this will scare any game away, so use your whistle only as a last resort."

"Will you be all right?" Desiree asked him.

Richard noted her concern for him. He acknowledged the same for her. "Yes, of course," he answered. He gave her a quick smile and rubbed her back.

They stepped back into the woods and then separated. Richard went to the left. He walked twenty feet, finding the forest heavily wooded, he moved closer to the meadow and went on. He went this way for ten minutes or so until he came to a small clearing. Bushes were growing partially around it, some of which still held withered berries. He stayed in the secluded woods, removed an arrow from its quiver, placed it onto the bowstring and then silently waited for his game.

After a while a doe cautiously entered the clearing. She made her way to the bushes. She gazed all around and studied her surroundings. Her nostrils opened widely as she smelled the air. Her ears searched for foreign sounds. She was of medium size. She moved again gracefully. Richard waited for the right moment. He pulled back his bowstring and then raised the bow. The doe became aware of him. She turned her head and stared at him with soft, brown eyes. Their eyes locked on one another. He sensed her energy.

Richard paused and loosened the arrow in his grip. Suddenly, there was a sharp pain in his thigh. He screamed loudly. The deer ran off. The agony overwhelmed him. He dropped to his knees and looked down. An arrow was sticking out above his right knee. Blood surrounded it. He leaned back into a sitting position. More pain came to him. He cried out once again in agony. Then he came to his senses. He reached into his coat pocket, found the whistle, put it to his mouth and blew it forcefully.

A man came out of the nearby woods. It was an old hunter. Gray hair stuck out beneath his hunter's cap and he had a gray moustache. There was an unusual bow in his hand. The bow had gold bosses and radiant ends.

"Are you all right," the man asked Richard when he was next to him. "I saw the deer and your reaction. That's when I let my arrow fly."

"I've got to get this arrow out of me!" Richard yelled at him.

"That will be difficult," the old hunter answered. "The tip is three bladed. To pull it out now would rip your leg open. It needs to be surgically removed."

Sam and Desiree arrived at the scene.

Desiree saw the protruding arrow. "Oh, Richard," she cried out.

Richard looked up at her. Their eyes met. She knelt down next to him. "It'll be all right. This is not life threatening," he told her. "It'll take an onslaught of arrows to take me out. I'll not give up this body until the sun moves north to the heavens," he shouted defiantly.

"Then we shan't part for a very long while," Desiree told everyone.

Richard's eyes pored over her. Her haunting beauty and seemingly inexhaustible desire captivated him. "Yes, that's the way it shall be," he answered.

Sam moved closer to Richard. "We have to do something about that arrow if we're going to get you out of here."

The old hunter knelt down next to Richard. Desiree stood up and moved away. The old man placed his hands down low on the arrow's shaft. Then he quickly snapped it off. Richard grimaced but held onto his pain.

"Desiree and I will get you out of here," Sam told him.

"Are you sure?" The old hunter said looking them over.

"We'll manage," Richard said. "My life's been in their hands for years."

"Very well," the huntsman said. "Here's my card should you ever have need of me."

The man handed the card to Richard. It was royal blue with gold lettering. Richard read it.

Gandiva Archery Unlimited. 'Realize the dream through us.' 'Bhishmatic Scoping Available.' Art Juna, Owner. Phone 773-726-2344.'

Richard placed the unusual card in his vest pocket. Sam and Desiree then helped him up. He placed an arm over each of their shoulders and they left the clearing. The old hunter watched the three of them disappear into the thick woods.

"What brings you by, Adam?" Sam and Ray were seating at Sam's office desk.

The room reeked of cigarette smoke; Adam cleared his nose. "I was wondering if you heard any more about Richard."

"He's back home now. He spent an extra night in Flagstaff for observation then got home yesterday. He's taking the day off and will back at work tomorrow," Sam said.

"Come and check this out," Ray requested.

Adam went over to the desk. An ashtray was overflowing, its ashes scattered everywhere. He leaned over and looked at the computer screen. Briefly he saw a reflection of Stewart Demaya. He turned and looked behind him, nobody was there. Looking back at the screen again he saw a nude woman. "Why that's Julie Mitchell," Adam exclaimed.

"Nice tits," Ray said. "These shots were taken before she became a big Hollywood star."

"Let's see if there's anything more graphic," Sam pleaded.

Ray backed out of the sight and went to a page with Julie Mitchell listings. He found one that said *Julie Mitchell Naughty Sex* and clicked on it. Several pictures came into view. He chose the most erotic one and zoomed in on it.

"I didn't know you could find this on the internet," Adam disclosed.

"Watch this," Ray said clicking under her picture.

A video began to play.

"You can get some good porn once you know what you're doing," Sam told him.

"You mean there's more of this?" Adam said.

"Sure," Sam responded. "You'd be surprised what some of these Hollywood stars have done to further their careers."

"There're plenty of gorgeous babes on these sights," Ray added.

Adam did not know what to think. Sex on the internet, he voiced to himself. What a crazy world we live in. You just can't get away from sex. "I've got to go, guys. Maybe I'll see you later in the break room."

Adam walked back to his office. He took a pile of papers from his desk's wire basket and then sat down with them. His mind wandered. He eyed two framed pictures that were on his right. He picked up one of them. It was a photo of him and Taneka standing on top of Mount Humphreys. Edwina had taken it with her digital camera. He and Taneka had been so happy. That's where they began their word play. Everything felt so good back then. And now what? He had ruined it or come close to ruining it. Almost two weeks and still there was no contact with her. When would she call him? He longed to speak to her now. He wanted to tell her how much he missed and needed her. He wanted to able to pledge his love to her.

Adam set the photo down. He reached out to take up the other picture, changed his mind, and instead stared at it. It was a photo of him in his green Cobra. Ray had snapped it one morning in Universal Holdings' parking lot. By possessing the Cobra one of his childhood dreams had been fulfilled. Owning it had given him pleasure. Now where was that pleasure? He was no longer poised on a mountain top with Taneka. The height of their joy had fallen to the level of a parking lot. What they had found in each other he could never purchase. It wasn't like a Cobra to be owned and possessed. What's found in another person may never be owned and possessed. One

219

simply shares the other's pleasure. Then, through love, they both grow together and it becomes a greater, unconditional love.

Adam's eyes fell on the paperwork in front of him. Two hours passed by in work. He felt hungry, reached into his desk, took out a protein bar and shoved it into his pocket. Then he left the office and went on to the break room.

Desiree was seated at a table with Jaya and Vicki drinking coffee. She saw him first. He wanted to get away. She beckoned him. He walked over to her.

"We were just talking about you," she told him.

Oh, God, he thought, what has she told them?

"Come and sit with us," Vicki requested. "I haven't seen much of you lately."

"Give me a moment; I need to get some water."

Adam returned shortly and sat down next to Vicki. Desiree was on the other side of the table. She studied him. It made him uncomfortable.

"What's new with you ladies?" He asked them.

Vicki and Jaya told Adam their latest news, Vicki's being the latest gossip. He wasn't interested. He was polite and pretended to listen. He couldn't. His mind was locked on the woman sitting across from him. What has she told Richard? Vicki and Jaya? He took out the protein bar.

"I see you eating those all the time," Vicki spoke out. "What do they taste like?"

Adam tore off a piece and gave it to her. She bit into it.

"Yuck. I don't know what you see in these," she cried out.

"Adam eats only what's good for him," Desiree declared.

"I eat what pleases me," Vicki responded. "Health has nothing to do with it."

"Adam's particularly fond of fruit," Desiree told her.

"What's your favorite?" Jaya wanted to know.

"Apples," Desiree answered for him.

Adam coughed. He was embarrassed and upset. Why is she like this? He asked himself. Doesn't she realize where things stand?

"Adam, Jaya's buying a cabin in Flagstaff," Desiree mentioned.

"That's nice," he said, happy with the subject change.

Jaya excitedly told everyone about her soon to be possession. She said she found the cabin on the day everyone went hunting. After a shopping spree in town she met with a local realtor and they went out and viewed three properties. When Sam returned from deer hunting she showed him pictures of the cabins. He left the final decision up to her. She was making an offer on her favorite one today.

"I hope it fits your needs," Adam said wondering why she never mentioned a thing about Richard's accident. The accident occurred the same day she had gone cabin hunting.

"It does. We'll all go up to Flagstaff over the Holidays and have a great time. Everyone can go skiing. We can even play in the snow and make snowmen."

"That sound like a lot of fun to me," Desiree said. "However, snowmen are a bit too soft for me. I like my men hard," she added looking Adam squarely in the eye.

Chapter 10

Winter

God promises a safe landing, not a calm passage.

It was mid-November and heavy snow had fallen in the high country. In less than two weeks the ski resorts would open for the Thanksgiving weekend. Sam and Jaya had already spent one weekend in their Flagstaff cabin and plans had been made for Adam, Ray, and Vicki to spend the upcoming holiday with them.

Adam and Taneka were still separated. They had spoken only once during the past month. A planned reconciliation had been arranged for Christmas Eve. Adam missed her terribly. In her absence he literally threw himself into his work. He tried reading worthwhile books, but his mind was just too restless and instead filled his spare time with outdoor magazines, movies and longer and more intense gym workouts.

At the age of sixteen Adam began lifting weights because he wanted to improve his athletic skills. He trained hard for five years. His past efforts explained why it was so easy for him to adapt to his present workouts. He was now putting in five or six days of training each week instead of the normal three. He chose to do a push-pull routine. One day he performed upper body exercises that pushed the weights away from him. This involved his chest, shoulders and triceps. The next day he did the opposite, he worked his back, biceps and forearms; the muscles used to pull the weight or resistance into the trainee. On the third day Adam worked his legs and abs. Each day's weight routine began with twenty minutes of cardio exercise on a treadmill, an elliptical machine, or a combination of both. His workouts had grown from sixty minutes to ninety.

Adam sought to put an end to a hectic day. He left the office early, hurried to his car, put the Cobra's top down, hopped in, and started the engine. He was on his way to the Mesa club. It was the closest Universal Fitness to the Karnan's home. Ray and Vicki were expecting him for dinner and Ray wanted to show off his car collection.

Adam finished his workout, showered quickly and then left the club and walked over to the nutritional store which was next to the gym.

"May I help you?" A young, muscular salesman asked Adam. The man was wearing a white T-shirt with the store's logo on it—a figure of an athlete flexing his bicep in one arm and with his other arm holding by his waist a canister of protein.

"Anything new in protein supplements?"

The salesman led him to a display table. "This one's pretty good. It's a blend of seven proteins," he said and picked up a large, red, see-through container.

"Does it contain enough L-Glutamine?"

The young man gave the container to Adam who then read its label. "This," he told the salesman, "is a good mixture of protein. Healthy, productive meals are somewhat like this. L-Glutamine is an important ingredient for assimilating supplemental proteins."

"Exactly," the clerk agreed. "What have you been using?"

"I've been taking the two leading brands for years," Adam answered. "I'll try this new product out and see if it helps me pack on muscle."

"Did you just come from the gym?"

"It was my push workout day," Adam told him.

"Do you need anything else? We have some new protein bars," the young man told him waving his hand out to a nearby shelf.

"Just this for now."

Adam paid the clerk and went out to his car. He set the protein canister on the seat next to him, put the key in the ignition, and then fired up the engine. Revving it twice, he let it idle down, then put the car into gear and sped off. In a short time he reached *Highway 60*, turned right and headed east. Twenty minutes later he found the Karnan's house and pulled into the drive. It was late in the afternoon.

Ray was standing next to a storage building about forty feet away from the driveway. He headed over to Adam and greeted him.

"I see my directions pointed you in the right direction. I sure do like that Cobra."

"Thanks," Adam said stepping out onto the driveway. "You should get one."

"Maybe next year you'll sell me yours. Vicki's in the house preparing dinner. I'll show you my car collection and then we'll join her."

Ray led Adam to the large building.

"This looks new."

"It was finished this fall. Now I have ample room for my collection. Vicki and I decided we didn't need to buy a new house. We have two and a half acres here. Putting up this big of a building was not a problem."

Ray opened the door and they went in. Six sports cars were in storage and there was room for more. Adam gave them a quick once over. Then he focused in on Ray's '62 Corvette. As he studied it he remembered in his youth how much he and his friends had drooled over that particular model.

"Ray, I love that Vette."

Soon the two of them began discussing the Corvette's history. When they were done Ray led Adam to the other cars.

"Ray, what's the attached roof for?" Adam asked when they went back outside. He was looking up at the building's extended roofing.

"It's for our RV."

"What RV?"

"Next year Vicki and I are getting one. That's why I have this cement pad we're standing on. Those are the RV hookups next to it," he said pointing at the ground next to the pad.

"Do you have a future trip planned?"

"Not yet, but we're definitely getting out of the heat as much as possible next summer."

"I don't blame you, the summers here are brutal. What about your boat?"

"That's now in storage up at Lake Roosevelt. We'll also keep it there when we take next year's trip."

"Living in the eastern part of the Valley puts you closer to the boat."

"It saves us about an hour's drive," Ray acknowledged. "Let's see if my wife has dinner ready."

Vicki came over and greeted them by the door. "Hi, Adam, I hope you're hungry. I fixed you chicken breasts and brown rice."

"Great, I'll gobble them up; I worked up a good appetite at the gym. How'd you know I'd like chicken and brown rice?"

"Ray told me. He overheard you and Richard at work talking about your meals."

"I remember that day. Ray came over and made faces at some of the food we mentioned. He didn't like me bum rapping beef and pork."

"I would've done the same," Vicki claimed.

"Adam says beef and pork have too much carbon and are harder to digest," Ray told her.

"That's right, Ray. They're also high in uric acid which can cause gout. We can only assimilate a small amount of uric acid each day. What's eaten in excess is stored in our body."

"What's wrong with that?" Vicki argued.

"It's not healthy. Because beef and pork are high in carbon it takes a lot of energy to digest them. This keeps us body conscious.

227

Also, these meats contain a high amount of deadly toxins. The animals are fed steroids, growth hormones, and other drugs. The slaughtered animal throws everything into its blood stream."

"This won't matter to Vicki. Will it?" Ray asked his wife.

"Damn right," Vicki snapped out.

"That's your choice," Adam concluded.

Vicki went over to oven to see if the chicken breasts were done. She cut into one of them. "Okay, we can dine now."

Ray and Adam took their places at the nearby dining table. Vicki brought out the meal and joined them.

As they ate they talked about travel. Ray mentioned the RV he wanted to buy. Vicki remarked that her husband always liked being at the helm of things, be it a boat, a car, or an RV. She said he was steering her into his desires. She didn't mind it, in fact, she rather liked it. These gave them pleasure and kept them away from life's tedious things."

After dinner they all retired to the family room. Adam sat in a dark tan, leather recliner. Ray and Vicki rested comfortably on a matching sofa. A teakwood coffee table was in front of it with knick-knacks, component remotes, and two stacks of magazines on top of it, one being *Better Homes & Gardens* and the other *Playboy.*

"Ray, I see you're an avid reader," Adam kidded pointing at the men's magazines.

"He likes *Better Homes & Gardens* best," Vicki said adding to the fun.

"Are you planning on going up to Sam and Jaya's cabin?" Ray asked Adam.

"I'll be there over the Thanksgiving weekend."

"Is Taneka coming with you?" Vicki asked him.

"They're still trying to work things out," Ray told her.

"Oh, I see. Well, I hope you work out whatever it is that needs working out."

"We will, Vicki," Adam claimed.

"Let's put on a movie," Ray suggested.

He stood up and went across the room to an entertainment center. Within the center was a large TV. It must have been at least seventy-two inches in screen size. Next to the set were a Blue Ray DVD player and a sound surround system. Several shelves were filled with CD's and DVD's. Ray selected a movie from one of the shelves, removed the disc from its case and placed it into the DVD player. When he was finished he returned to the sofa, picked up a remote from the teak table and began playing the movie.

The film co-starred Julie Mitchell. Adam recognized one of the scenes; it was the actress's nude shot he recently had seen in Sam's office with Ray.

It was nearly eleven o'clock. Adam thanked the Karnan's for the evening and then both he and Ray went outside to the Cobra. The temperature had dropped and the air was cool so Adam put the top up on the car.

"I'm definitely going to get a Cobra to add to my collection," Ray told him after he was done.

Adam opened the car's door, got in, and sat down on the bucket seat. "You've got good taste, Ray. I wouldn't mind having your '62 Corvette."

"Maybe you should get one."

"With what? This car's already depleted my savings."

"Don't worry; you're in with Demaya now, the money will come," Ray claimed.

"Yeah, I suppose so. I'll see you Monday."

Ray watched him pull out of the drive and race down the highway. When the Cobra was out of sight he went back into the house to his wife.

The weekend's freeway traffic was heavy. Adam decided to go into the highway's middle lane where the cars flowed at a steady. He began thinking about Taneka. Another evening had slipped by without her by his side. He was making new friends but they were doing little to satisfy his needs. If he had been with Taneka this night the two of them would have gone out for dinner, gone onto the movies or else returned to his house and watched one. Either way they would have ended up talking and cuddling at his or her place. The evening would have been time spent enjoying life instead of an attempt at it.

Upon arriving home Adam quickly went to his study and turned on his laptop. He had hopes of finding new messages on the screen. There were none. He wanted to send one now but knew Taneka didn't want that. It would be a mistake if he pushed things. No, he better not rock the boat. He had to stay on course for another five weeks. So he shut down his email site and thought about something else. The four day Thanksgiving break was quickly approaching. He would leave early Thursday morning for Sam and Jaya's cabin, stay a couple of days and ski at the Snowbowl. Wrapped around the skiing would be socializing, card playing, and whatever else could keep him busy. There would just be the two couples and himself at the Flagstaff chalet. This made him the odd man out. The others knew he was having a problem, that's probably why he had been invited.

Adam was fully aware that Holidays spent in the absence of family or friends were often lonely, and that was his predicament now. He had no steady companion, no one to be close to, no one to really talk to. Taneka wasn't going to be there. Why? He had yet to learn self-control that's why. Sure the sexual instinct was strong in him, how many males could say otherwise? What kind of excuse is that? He and Taneka were close. They had their fun occasionally. They weren't sexually over active. They truly loved one another.

Five more weeks, Adam thought. Just five more weeks and then he would make everything up to her. They would go ahead with their summer wedding. Their best friends, Harish and Edwina would be there. He wished they were here now. They'd talk to Taneka on his behalf and then he wouldn't have to wait five long weeks to see her.

Adam checked the time. It was nearly midnight and he should be in bed. Unbeknownst to him, something had entered the room, something that was dark and foreboding. It slowly crept over to Adam. Then part of it projected out and found its way into his mind. Like a seed the projection began germinating. It spread out and then became part of Adam's thoughts, a part where habits are formed and actions instigated.

The laptop in front of Adam was still on. There had been another actress in the movie he had seen earlier at the Karnan's home, Pamela Johnson. She was sexy, built, and attractive. Adam clicked on her website. * * *

231

The remaining days leading to the holiday break found Adam occupied with work, weights and women. Once work duties were completed, he drove to the gym, exercised heavily, returned home, showered, ate and then watched a recorded show or a rented movie. Serious reading was of no avail. It was easier to park in front of the 'box.' Then, before retiring, it was time for that other thing. It was time to water the dark plant growing within him. Another actress he had seen on the evening's 'box' spiked his interest. What kind of body did she have? What was she like nude? He thought these explorations were harmless. It started out simply enough. First there were nude photos, then actual videos. This led to further investigations. Two hours quickly passed by, half of which were videos. He didn't intend for this to happen, it just did, much like it had with Desiree.

What was behind these dark impulses? What drove him to fulfill them? It was all a mistake. He knew that. After three nights of restless, erotic sleep, enough was enough. Anything affecting his health had to go. And, most definitely, anything affecting his relationship with Taneka must vanish.

Adam found his strength in health. Sleep and exercise were two of his priorities. While in college Adam had experimented with marijuana. Food had tasted so good then. He thought if this sense were heightened maybe another sense would be. Maybe his workouts would be better. So he smoked a joint, went to the gym, and nearly killed himself. He lost control of a heavily weighted barbell. That pissed him off; he had no balance, thus he was forced to put an end to the workout. He had just wasted a day of training and also thrown off his routine. So that was the end of the marijuana. It wasn't a difficult decision. He had observed how much his friends changed with the use of that drug. They became more selfish and self-centered with each week's passing. He didn't want to be like that. So he changed his friends and quit his marijuana experimentation.

And cigarettes? They tasted awful, were meaningless, and thus were out. Alcohol threw his body off. After a few hangovers he limited all drinking to an occasional non-alcoholic beer.

So, with all this in mind, the time, Adam knew, had come for him to quit this uncontrolled internet hunting. With a gritty effort he made his way through the tangled dark plant growing within him, found his hidden will power, and pulled it out of the plant's entwining roots.

Ten o'clock Thanksgiving morning Adam parked his SUV alongside the Karnan's car. He grabbed his duffle bag, stepped out of the car and made his way through the snow to their chalet.

Sam greeted him at the door. "You're right on time, where's your ski gear?"

"I left it in the car. No sense moving it twice," Adam answered.

"Come on in."

Adam kicked the snow off his boots. Seeing a mat by the door, he removed his boots and placed them alongside the others that were there.

Jaya came over and welcomed him. When they were done with their greetings she led him to the guest bedroom at the end of a long hallway. Adam set his bag on top of the room's dresser. "Nice cedar chalet," he told her.

"It is nice." Jaya said. "I'll show you the rest of it now."

The tour ended in the great room. The room had a high, vaulted ceiling. There were large full length windows to the north that offered a spectacular view of the snow covered San Francisco Peaks. Several evergreen trees stood on the grounds outside the windows. Clumps of snow, like sparkling ornaments, hung from the trees' branches and gave the appearance of a Christmas tree filled field. Within the great room, a fire burned from a corner fireplace. Two ceiling fans pushed its rising heat back down making the room quite comfortable and cozy.

"Adam, sit down and rest awhile," Jaya told him. "The other guests will be here shortly, and then all of you can head up to the Snowbowl."

Adam nodded at the other couple in the room. "Ray and Vicki are here, who else are you referring to?"

"Richard and Desiree."

"I thought they weren't coming," Adam said somberly.

"They changed their plans," Jaya responded. "They'll be staying three nights."

"Oh, I see," Adam replied softly.

That other couple arrived twenty minutes later. Soon thereafter, after everything was in order, all but Jaya left for the ski resort. She wasn't interested in skiing; instead she stayed behind and prepared the Thanksgiving meal.

The six skiers traveled in two cars to the Snowbowl. It took them nearly a half hour to drive the seven miles to the lodge.

The Snowbowl is built on the San Francisco Mountains at an elevation of ninety-two hundred feet. The resort has two lodges.

There are five lifts. One lift takes it occupants up over eleven thousand, five hundred feet. In the background mountain peaks rise over twelve thousand feet, the largest being Mount Humphreys, Arizona's highest.

The party broke into three pairs. Ray went with Adam, and Sam went off with Richard. The two women wished to ski together.

Adam and Ray waited for the others to leave. Since Ray was a novice skier Adam led him to the slope's easiest run. When they arrived there they found a long line of skiers waiting for the chairlift that would take them to the top of the ski run.

"How many runs are there here, Adam?"

"Forty," he replied. "The uppermost starts way up there," Adam said pointing his gloved hand at it.

"How high is that?"

"I believe it's well over eleven thousand feet. We're fortunate today. There's only a trace of wind. When you're comfortable, after a couple of runs, we'll go on to more challenging courses."

"I'm game," Ray declared.

They skied for nearly two hours. Ray became tired and hungry so he and Adam went to the main lodge. They bought sandwiches and beverages then made their way into the eating area. The picnic-like tables in the room were mostly occupied.

Adam spotted Desiree and Vicki sitting at a table near the far wall. Desiree stood out like a sore thumb. She was easily the prettiest and sexiest woman in the room. Her long, black, silken hair and sensual face accentuated by those green eyes reached out to Adam.

"There are the girls, we'll go join them," Adam told Ray.

"Back already," Vicki said as the men approached the table.

"We're hungry and need to rest," Adam answered.

Vicki's freckled face broke into a smile. "Then you better sit down and join us."

Adam and Ray sat down on the opposite side of the table. Above them, high up on the wall, a television was on and a game was being broadcast. The Lions and Packers' were playing their traditional Thanksgiving football game.

Ray glanced at the television briefly and then looked at the two women. "Have you seen Rich and Sam?"

"Not yet," Vicki answered.

"They're probably chasing snow bunnies," Desiree alleged.

Vicki began talking and soon three of them were engaged in conversation.

Adam remained silent and in the background. He studied them as they spoke. Desiree, he said to himself, has a sensual energy; everything she does is an expression of it. Vicki has a slender figure that is rather rigid, her mannerisms minimal. Vicki is childlike cute, Desiree is all out gorgeous. Ray is obviously attracted to her; he's barely taking his eyes off her. Vicki seems nonplussed by it. Apparently she's used to it.

Adam put his thoughts behind him and began watching the football game on the set above him.

"Here are the boys now," Desiree yelled out.

Sam was across the way with Richard who was next to him limping. Desiree stood up and hurriedly went to him.

"Rich, what's wrong with your leg?" Desiree asked him.

"He's skied too many runs today," Sam answered for Richard.

"I'll help you to the table, Rich," Desiree offered.

"I can make it on my own, Luv."

Desiree knew when to let him be. "All right, let's go to the table."

Richard followed her and sat down next to her. He wanted lunch. Desiree, Vicki and Sam left for the snack bar.

"Who's winning, Adam?" Richard asked looking up at the game.

"As usual, the Packers are beating the Lions," Adam told him.

"Then it's going to be another bad Thanksgiving for Detroit," Richard concluded.

Desiree, Vicki, and Sam came back shortly carrying sandwiches, chips and beer.

"Let's go into the bar, have a few more drinks and watch the game from there," Richard told them.

"I'm going out for a smoke first," Sam answered.

Sam left the lodge and Ray went into the adjoining room with Richard. Adam stayed with the women.

"Why didn't you go with them? Richard won't bite you," Desiree said.

"That's right, Adam," Vicki added. "Rich is open-minded."

Desiree saw the look of concern on Adam's face. "It's all right, he doesn't know about us."

"And if it did what would it matter?" Vicki claimed.

"Wait a minute," Adam said staring hard at Desiree. "You told her."

Desiree fixed her eyes on him then laughed. "Didn't you hear Vicki? She said it doesn't matter. She won't mention it to anyone."

"That's right," Vicki agreed. She leaned over closer to him. "It was just sex. Desiree wanted your body and you wanted hers. You're not married and so what if you are," she added shrugging her shoulders.

"Is that a justification?" He asked her.

"It is to me," Vicki answered. "Richard does his own thing as you well know. Everybody knows about Ashley. The thing is this, he comes back to Desiree and she does the same to him. They have each other. So what if they have their little flings."

"Adam, stop getting worked up over what happened," Desiree spoke out. "We had fun. We enjoyed each other. That's life. It's as simple as that."

"It hasn't been that simple for me," he responded. 'I've lost my fiancé."

"You haven't lost her. Taneka's a big girl. She needs to put everything in the right perspective. Once she balances it all out she'll come back to you. After all it's not like we're running off together."

"Desiree has a good point," Vicki claimed. "Ray has his nights out from time-to-time. He likes his pleasure. As long as he's good to me why should I care?"

"What about loyalty, Vicki? You're married. Shouldn't there be a special bond for you, why the need for another sexual partner?" Adam argued.

"There's no right or wrong. I do what I like, so should you. We should get whatever we want. End of discussion."

"You and Desiree have your ways and I have mine," Adam informed her and then made a mental note—he must try harder, use his will, and change his ways.

"Vicki and I know what we want," Desiree claimed forcefully breaking Adam's concentration.

Adam stared at her. "But is that giving you lasting happiness?" He retorted calmly.

The skiers returned to the chalet late in the afternoon. After partaking of a traditional Thanksgiving meal the evening was spent drinking, card playing, and socializing. When the talk had become boisterous Adam retired to his room.

The next day the four men ventured back to the ski mountain, again traveling in two cars. The women stayed at the cozy cabin. By mid-afternoon Adam had had enough skiing and drove back alone to the cabin.

"Adam, where's everybody?" Jaya asked him seeing he was alone.

"They're staying longer. When I left they were in the bar watching a collegiate football game," Adam answered.

"I bet that's not all they're watching," Vicki let known.

"Jaya, they said to tell you they'd be eating and hanging out at the lodge."

"That means we won't see them all that soon," Desiree conveyed.

"Well, Adam, it looks like you have the three of us all to yourself," Vicki said without looking at him.

"Will you be able to control yourself with three gorgeous women?" Desiree said teasing him.

"If that's possible amongst sirens," Adam responded.

"What kind do you mean, the kind that whirl on tops of cars or the kind that run free and seduce?" She asked grinning impishly.

"We're dining in one hour," Jaya burst out ending their word play. "We're having leftovers. There's one piece of pumpkin pie left and that's mine," she told them decisively.

It was after ten. Adam said goodnight to the three women and went to his room. He wasn't interested in their small talk. Earlier in the evening the four of them had watched television, Jaya chose every program. Growing tired of the shows everyone had moved closer to the warm fireplace. Once there, the women gossiped, consumed wine, and talked women things.

Adam changed into his PJ's and then sat down on the edge of the queen size bed. He looked over at the night stand next to him, saw an outdoor magazine lying on top of it and picked it up. He reclined comfortably onto the two pillows braced behind him. He was tired but not sleepy so he began skimming through the magazine. He found an article along with pictures of the John Muir Trail in the Sierra Madre Mountains. The article made him think of his friends.

Maybe next year, Taneka and I can go there, he said to himself. Harish and Edwina can join us. Simple pleasures are the most enjoyable. Why, then, have I made my life so complex? I'm my own worst enemy; it isn't Stewart, Desiree, all those others, or life's obstacles. It's me. I've used my freewill wrongly. Everything I've done has come back to me.

Who put those obstacles, the trials, tribulations and other tests in front of me? Harish told me that pain is the love cry used by God to bring His lost children back to Him. Pain, is a great motivator. Who is it that sets God's love cries into motion? We do. We don't use our free will properly. We err and harm ourselves.

Adam finished reading the article and then placed the magazine back on the night stand, dimmed the lamp and stretched out on the bed. He rested there and tried to sleep. Ten minutes passed this way and then the bedroom door opened. Desiree stood in the doorway. She was wearing only a revealing negligee. She began walking towards him. Behind and silently following her was something dark, something without shape and solidity. Adam saw only the scantily clad Desiree.

"What are you doing?" He asked Desiree irritably.

"I'm lonesome," she answered and sat down next to him.

"You shouldn't be here," he said looking at the clock next to the lamp. It was after eleven.

"Richard's not home yet," Desiree said pouting.

"Aren't the girls keeping you company?"

"No. They went off to their rooms."

"You should be in yours."

"I'm not. I'm here with you."

"Look, Desiree, we had an encounter. I'm not Richard."

"I'm horny," she told him and then climbed above him. The looseness of her gown exposed her perfect 38's.

"Don't do this, Desiree."

"Shush," she said putting her hand over his mouth. "Aren't you horny?"

He pushed her hand away. "I haven't had sex since you and I were together. I don't want it now."

She sat up and was once again looking down at him. "Don't you desire me?"

"That's one of my problems. I do want you physically," he admitted.

"What's your other problem?"

"I want a loving and lasting relationship. I can't have them with you."

"I'm not here for love. I'm here for sex."

"I'm glad you've noticed the difference between the two."

"So it doesn't matter then. We simply enjoy each other's body. Sex is a natural act. There doesn't have to be any consequences."

"Maybe that's true for you. It's not for me. We can stop this now. All we have to do is use our will and self-control."

The darkness behind Desiree increased. They did not see it. Desiree placed her hand on Adam's thigh near his manhood.

"Your desire for me is stronger than your willpower," she told him.

"I'm not that weak," he said making no effort of removing her hand.

"Is that so? Then why do you have that hard-on?"

"Because you're such a damn attractive woman."

"Then take me now."

"I can't."

"You can enjoy me now or you can play with yourself later."

"That's unfair."

She pulled off her negligee and threw it onto the floor.

The thing, the darkness that was near Adam and Desiree took shape, and from that shape a substance formed; the substance projected itself into the two of them, consumed them and made them feel that all that was important, all that was desired, was possible now by an action of lust.

"Here we go again," Adam said weakly.

Desiree nodded wickedly, tore off Adam's clothing, and they heatedly gave of one another.

Desiree collapsed on top of Adam, their action of lust completed. They held on to one another briefly and then she moved away from him, stepped out onto the floor and gathered up her negligee. Glancing back she said, "Thanks for the nightcap, Adam," and then she slid her garment over her head and down over her body.

"Let's not tell anyone about this," he requested.

"It will be our secret," she promised.

"I still want to get back with Taneka."

"Don't worry about our play, Adam. It was just a biological act."

"I think you're wrong. There's more to sex than that."

"Think what you like. Goodnight, Adam."

Desiree quizzedly looked about the room, grimaced as if she should be aware of something, then pranced out of the room.

Adam also felt something odd about the room, as if he weren't alone now. He also glanced about him but saw nothing that could account for the strangeness he was feeling. He shook his head, stepped out of bed and then went into the bathroom. Standing in front of the sink he began washing himself.

Watching Adam from within the dim light of the bedroom was Stewart Demaya! Demaya smiled devilishly. He knew he had imprisoned another soul within his world. His use of Desiree had sealed that for him.

A mist formed around Demaya's smile, grew until it covered him completely, and then both he and the mist were gone.

After his attempt of making himself clean Adam returned to the bedroom. He climbed into bed and waited for sleep to overtake him. His waiting was fruitless. The evening, its strangeness, and his uncontrolled desires kept playing over and over in his mind. The guilt and shame he was feeling would not leave him.

Adam rose early the next morning, dressed quickly, packed his bag, and went out to the great room. Nobody was up and about so he wrote a note saying he was cutting his weekend short. He placed the note on the dining table and then went out to his car. He placed his bag on the seat next to him, started the engine and sped off leaving the chalet behind him. Soon he reached the heart of Flagstaff and turned onto the interstate. Two and a half agonizing hours later he arrived home. It was eight thirty. He was frustrated, lost, and depressed. After parking in the garage, he grabbed his belongings then went into the house and on to the kitchen. He threw his bag on the counter, went to the refrigerator, grabbed a bottle of protein and sat down at the counter.

His thoughts were wild. His life was chaos. What's going on with me? He asked himself. It isn't just sex. What's causing my restlessness? Why can't I resist Desiree? Am I that weak? Why does that desire run so strongly throughout my mind?

What had appeared delightful to Adam's senses was developing into a bed of poison and leading him towards disaster. Pain from it, like powerful pistons, was punctuating the chamber of his peace. He had become a puppet. The strings of his habits, emotions, passions, and senses were making him dance to their bidding, shackling his soul to the earthly wheel. He always thought he had unlimited freedom and free choice, yet he had failed to see the binding poison building within him.

He had to change his ways; he had to stop the poison from spreading further. Everything was at risk, especially Taneka. He needed to do something about their relationship now. He would try a new approach; he would send her flowers this very day.

Adam went into his study, turned on the laptop, clicked on the internet, and began searching for a local florist. He found one, took out his cell phone from his pants pocket and called the number listed for the florist. A woman answered. He ordered a dozen red roses, gave the woman the address for their delivery and told her to sign it 'Miss you, Tan. Love, Adam.' The woman took down his debit card information and then the call was ended. Adam went back to the computer and checked his email. There was none. Four more weeks, he thought, four more weeks. * * *

Twenty-eight days, that's how much time remained for Adam to change himself, to do the inner work needed for the reconciliation with Taneka.

Although his will had been weakened by Desiree there still was a strength left in Adam. Perhaps this strength is what Demaya was after? Adam had reached the low point in his life. If he was going to change had to do it now. With a new determination Adam began tackling the task of inner transformation.

Adam stopped hunting for sexually stimulating sites on the internet. Fortunately, the mental seeds of this habit had not yet germinated within him. He used his 'won't power' to prevent their growth. Harish once told him 'won't power' was a method he personally used for keeping out of harm's way.

Adam learned from his recent experiences that the sense of sight is easily stimulated. How could he change this? How could he learn to see women in a nonsexual way? The world is full of sexual stimulation. It's found in advertisements, television, movies, clothing and elsewhere. Eliminating sexual attraction wasn't going to be easy. Perhaps visualizing women as mothers or sisters would work. That method might help him overcome his problem.

Adam's efforts over the remaining twenty eight days reinforced his willpower and added to his inner strength. Within this time frame he made a continual commitment to improve himself with everything that came his way. First, there was work. He visited the Universal Fitness clubs, observed each one's atmosphere and listened to the needs of the staff and the customers. Then, after work, he frequented the library where he checked out self-help books authored by Paolo Coelho, Don Miguel Ruiz. He read *Journey of Souls* and *Destiny of*

Souls, two fascinating books concerning case studies about reincarnation and life between lives. The books were authored by Michael Newton a clinical psychologist.

In early December, Adam was invited out to dinner by Dinar and Melia. He went to the restaurant that night expecting to find only the two of them. Much to his surprise there was a third person at their table. Dinar had invited Kory, Adam's former girlfriend. She was pretty, and there were hopes all-around of her winning him back. (It was Stewart Demaya's idea. He was aware of Adam's new found 'won't power' so he cleverly set Kory up as bait hoping to break Adam's will once and for all.) However, Kory was history to Adam. Their relationship had gone as far as it could go. Adam wanted something more meaningful. He had other needs. There was no love, romance, or bond between them and he was determined to keep it that way.

Kory asked Adam to drive her home after the dinner. Out of courtesy, he did so. Upon their arrival she invited him in. He politely refused. She told him that she missed him but not to worry, she wasn't seeking a commitment. She told him she missed their great sex, and, for old time's sake, wanted him to make love to her now. He said that wasn't possible. Then he told himself that having sex with Kory would be like having sex with Desiree. It wasn't making love, it was making sex. He wanted love. So Adam reached within himself, used his new found 'won't power,' and ended the evening. (Unbeknownst to him this act of strength added greatly to Demaya's displeasure). * * *

At five thirty sharp Adam was on Taneka's doorstep. It was Christmas Eve, the appointed day of their reunion. He knocked on the door. She opened it.

"Hello, Adam."

"You look so good," he replied. She let him kiss her lightly. "I've really missed you, Tan. It's been an agonizingly long time."

She put her hand in his. "Let's go for a walk."

"Where?"

"At the park, we'll drive there and then walk."

"All right," he said.

After a short drive Adam parked the car in the park's lot and then helped Taneka out. They held hands and walked across the grass, now brown in winter dormancy. Palm trees, thirty feet in height, surrounded the grounds. The afternoon was cool yet comfortable. They came to a walkway and followed it. Adam let go of Taneka's hand and put his arm around her. They strolled along talking of their past. They mentioned Harish and Edwina and how much they missed them. Coming to a bench near a playground they sat upon it. Several children were in the playground. The younger ones frolicked in the sand and slid down the slides while the older ones occupied the swings and monkey bars. Two of the older children, a boy and a girl, were on a teeter-totter trying to find its balance.

"I want it to go back to the way it was," Adam told Taneka.

"I wish that also."

"When can we be a couple again?"

"That depends."

"On what?"

"It depends on whether or not you're going to be faithful to me."

"Tan, I love you. I've always loved you. Isn't that enough?"

"I know you love me. I've missed you and have wanted to be with you. What I don't want is another woman in the middle."

"There isn't, Tan. I know what I've done has hurt you."

"Have you gotten over your urges, Adam?"

"What do you mean?"

"You know what I mean."

Adam's face stiffened and along with it wore his action of lust like a garment of guilt.

"Tan, I have something I better tell you."

"You've done something wrong," she said loudly. "I see it all over you."

He looked away from her. He tried to speak, broke down, and then it all came out. He told her what had happened again with Desiree.

"What!" Taneka exclaimed.

"I know it was wrong. I'm just being honest with you. I love you. I don't want to keep any secrets from you."

"Love is not associated with selfish desires," she retorted.

"I wasn't trying to be selfish. Desire just overtook me," Adam tried to explain.

"You need to keep that desire in your pants. Now I know why your penis has a whole at the end of it, it's for getting oxygen to your brain!" She shouted hotly.

"Look, I know I'm weak that way. I promise you it won't happen again. I won't let it. I'm changing. I will overcome this as well as all my other desires." Adam assured her of this and then went on and told her about his encounter with Kory and how he had turned down her offer of sex.

"And that's supposed to make a difference now? We can't go on like this. You have to overcome your desires and restlessness, Adam. I would've left five minutes ago if I didn't care about you. But I do care. However, I cannot and will not live with the uncertainty of your loyalty. You must learn the meaning of love. That's something I can't teach you. Go find it out. Go out into the world and take its hard knocks. Maybe you'll lift the cloud covering your soul and realize the nature of love and the true nature of soulmates. As it is now, I can't be with you. You must find out what real values are. I want you to take me home now."

"Can't we work this out together?" Adam pleaded.

"Not in this lifetime," Taneka concluded fighting hard to hold back her tears.

"I wish you hadn't said that," he said sadly.

She rose from the bench. "Let's go."

He stood up and they began walking back to the car. Along the way they passed the playground, empty now except for two children. A boy was on his knees. He was using his hands to dig at the sand beneath him. A girl sat at the sand's edge watching him.

This was the hardest and sadist winter of Adam's life. He was desperately in need of help. Somehow, someway, he had to gather all his strength and rise above the trials and tribulations he had created. He needed Taneka's loving understanding and Harish's wisdom if he was going to successfully free himself from his weaknesses. The distance between him and Taneka had become greater than ever. So that left Harish to supply the needed helping hand. And that was another problem of distance. His friend was miles away on the other side of the world. All Adam could do was to try and recall Harish's wisdom and work with that. That's all he ever could do. Harish had told him once that another person may teach or tell you how to change, but you have to be the one that actually does the work.

What exactly did he have to change? Adam had to free himself from desires and attractions to the opposite sex. He also had to free himself from desiring unnecessary possessions.

Adam needed neutrality to reach the state of pure feeling, to reach the state of non-judgment that was free from prejudice and emotion. If he were to ever acquire the greatest of all love for Taneka, divine love, he had to make the supreme effort of overcoming all his deficiencies. He had to be stronger than the environment around him.

Adam had his work cut out for him, work that could only be done from the inside out.

Chapter 11

The Inner Work

Until established in his true Being man cannot possibly know peace.

"Where's Taneka?" Edwina asked.

Adam was at Sky Harbor Airport. "I'll tell you about that later," he answered.

"I hope everything is all right," Harish commented.

"Let's go pickup your bags," Adam told them leading them to the stairway.

They walked down the stairs to the lower floor, and on to their designated baggage carousel. They waited a few minutes and then Harish and Edwina's luggage arrived. The men each grabbed a bag and made their way through the terminal an on to Adam's car. Edwina followed them.

"I've missed you guys," Adam said after they were settled in the car. "It's been five months since we've been together. How was your trip?"

"We had a splendid time, especially India," Edwina informed him.

"You must be tired. You've a half days' time difference to adjust to."

'It has been a long day of travel," Harish admitted.

"Then I better take you straight home."

"Adam, I want to know about Taneka," Edwina requested.

"That's a long story. After you've rested come over to my house tomorrow. We'll have an early meal and talk then."

Adam led Harish and his sister to his back patio. It was two o'clock in the afternoon. The sky was cloudless and blue. A light, soothing breeze swept through the yard; Camelback Mountain dominated the view to the north. Eight trees, four Palms and four Mesquite, were spaced evenly around the yard's perimeter. Crushed rock of assorted desert colors as well as a variety of desert plants filled most of the yard's landscape. At the edge of the brick patio near where the three friends were sitting three gardenia bushes gave off their fragrance.

A light conversation began and then Edwina grew serious and asked about Taneka. Adam mumbled a few words.

"What are you trying to say?" Edwina asked him.

Adam composed himself and then out came the whole story.

"Oh, Adam, how could you?" Edwina said sadly.

"I know I was wrong. I just couldn't stop myself," he admitted.

"Harish, you need to help him," Edwina pleaded.

"Do you want my help, Adam?"

"At this point I'll take all the help I can get."

"Have you tried meditating?"

"I'm too restless for that. My mind goes everywhere."

"That's natural for everyone. In your present state it's become even harder. Don't be discouraged. Meditation takes practice and patience. When we try focusing our minds on one thing we soon become aware of our uncontrolled thoughts. We constantly talk to ourselves. We must learn to shut off this interior dialogue. When a jar filled with water and sand is shaken the sand distorts the water. Set the jar down, and, one by one, each sand particle falls to the bottom and the water becomes clear again. The sand particles in the jar are our thoughts, the water our minds. Gradually, the thoughts, like the sand, will fall away due to our one pointed concentration."

"What should I concentrate on, Harish?"

"You should concentrate on God or one of His aspects. If you want peace, love, or wisdom, focus on one of them."

"What do you do?"

"I do what I've just told you. I also practice meditation techniques which help me calm my breath and shut off my sense telephones. I'm trying to be aware of my oneness with God or else I try to feel His Presence through a saint, a Master, or a Divine Attribute."

"How can I get rid of my current difficulties, Harish?"

"Adam, you must do the inner work. Nobody can do that for you. It isn't enough to just live a good life. Life is about problems and overcoming them. There are four things we can do to defeat our difficulties. First, we must have faith in God. He will see us through our trials and will never give us more than we can handle. Secondly, we must meditate deeply. We must pray for God's guidance and help. Thirdly, we have to surrender to the will of God. Finally, we must relax and let go of our problem. Give it to God."

"And this is where I fight the good fight," Adam declared.

"That's the right way of looking at it. In *The Bhagavad Gita*, Krishna advises his devotee Arjuna to ask at the end of each day, 'How did they?' This means, at day's end, the spiritual warrior asks, 'how did I do in my inner battle of defeating the enemies that keep me ego conscious and unaware of my perfect soul.' The answers that come from this practice will help us in our quest for self-improvement."

"I should write all of this down," Adam said.

"I'll put the points we've covered in writing and give them to you the next time we meet. You and I will come up with a battle plan. You want Taneka back. Edwina and I will help you.

"Adam, I'll talk to Taneka and try to reason with her," Edwina promised.

"Be gentle. I don't want to rock her boat any more than I already have."

"I will, Brother."

The next day Edwina met with Taneka. Taneka made tea and they visited in her apartment's small living room. They talked about Edwina's travel and then Taneka, without any coaxing rom Edwina, spoke of the broken relationship with Adam. She began to cry and Edwina comforted her.

"Tan, I can understand your feelings," Edwina said sympathetically. "Adam didn't act in the best interest for either of you. But know this; he greatly regrets what he has done. He's trying hard to overcome his shortcomings."

"I've lost faith in him. Do you know what it's like to completely put your trust in someone and then be let down by that person?"

"I can only imagine what it's like."

"It's very painful. I care about Adam, but I can't have him the way he is."

"Taneka, love is the mirror that reflects both the good and bad traits of both of you. Try and see Adam's good traits. You two have something special. Don't let the past spoil that. Love means being willing to forgive."

"I don't know if that's possible," Taneka claimed. "Everything's so hard now."

"Tan, you and Adam are more than lovers, you are also friends. Friends are always there to help one another. Adam needs your friendship now more than ever. You should help him work out his problems. Look at this as a way of growing spiritually strong together. See it as a way of surpassing human love with divine love. Please, do both yourselves a favor. Get back in touch with Adam."

"I'll consider seeing Adam as a friend," she said remotely.

"That's a start. Think everything out now. Try to remember that only the good and beautiful are true and living. The bad and ugly are only the shadow of what is." * * *

Adam waited expectantly by the phone waiting for it to ring. It was Saturday morning. While he waited he went over to his study's bookcase and scanned a shelf that contained what he called 'his special books.' He found the A*utobiography of a Yogi*, by Paramahansa Yogananda. Harish had actually given it to him during their college days. Adam never read it at the time; his life had been too full of academic, social, and athletic activities. He sat down by his desk with the book and read into the third chapter and then his cell phone rang. Quickly he answered it. It was Edwina. She told him what had transpired between her and Taneka and that things looked encouraging. Her words made his heart feel lighter. Finally there was a ray of hope, and something to look forward to.

After they finished their conversation, Adam went into the kitchen and made lunch. An hour passed by then Harish arrived carrying a notebook. The two of them went out to the back patio and settled there. Adam mentioned the book he had begun reading earlier.

"So you've kept *The Autobiography of a Yogi* after all these years," Harish said. "I referred to it last fall when we were at Lake Tahoe."

"I know, that's when you explained the Adam and Eve story. You said you discovered its meaning in that book."

"That particular work by Paramahansa Yogananda has done wonders for many, many spiritual searchers," Harish claimed.

"I never got into the book when I was in college," Adam admitted.

"You weren't ready for it then. Evidently it meant something to you. You've kept it all these years."

"I suppose so. Do you think it will help me now?"

"Absolutely, don't take it lightly."

"Is its content true or just something the author made up?"

"Adam, you'll have to be the judge of that. Ask yourself questions about you've read and then decide for yourself which answers are right."

"Wise council, my friend, I'll follow your advice."

"Here are the notes I promised you the other day," Harish said handing his notebook over to Adam.

"Thanks, do you want me to keep this?"

"It's for you. Use it as you see fit."

"What are we going to discuss today?"

"The inner work involves variety of subjects. Everyone has lessons to learn and psychological kinks to remove," Harish claimed.

"I don't know if I'm going to like this," Adam declared.

"The progress of a yogi is in direct proportion to his ability to endure the pain of transformation."

"This means facing my faults and working through them," Adam said.

"Yes, that is so. Unfortunately, our errors have subjected us to repeated deaths and rebirths. We have turned our world into a nightmare."

"An ongoing bad dream."

"Nobody wants to admit that he has faults. However, the sooner we admit and face them, the sooner we will advance on the spiritual path. Remember, a Master became a Master by mastering himself. Our imperfect state is only temporary. Our soul is made in the image of God. He is perfect thus we are perfect. We are not the body or the ego. We must remove the dirt of delusion covering our soul if we are to discover our true nature."

Harish told Adam to look at the notes he was holding. As he did so, Harish gave a brief review of each one. When he was finished he asked Adam how his meditations were coming along.

Adam sighed. "I don't know if you could call them meditations. My mind is full of thoughts and I am so restless."

"It will take practice. Just keep your attention here," Harish said placing a finger between his eyebrows."

"I'll do my best, Harish."

"That's all anyone can do, Adam. Doing our best means doing the best we can at that moment. Our best varies with circumstances."

"Then we shouldn't be hard on ourselves," Adam added.

"We should never be hard on ourselves. We simply work at the best of our abilities at the present time."

"What should I do about my bad habits and temptations?"

"To begin with, you must introspect. Look at your negative and positive points. How did you get them? How did you become what you are? You must remove your bad traits and sow seeds of spiritual qualities. Concentrate on the opposite good habit. That will help you remove the bad one.

"Develop 'won't power.' Simply say no to what's tempting you and walk away from it. Use your will. Willpower consists of desire and enthusiasm. To change we must desire to change and we must do this enthusiastically. Divert your mind to some good habit and make it part of you.

"Anything that strengthens your mind is your friend. Anything that weakens your mind is your enemy. Watch the environment you are in. This means people, books, movies, and associates. Surround yourself with what's good and wholesome.

"We must learn to behave. We must do what we are supposed to do when we are supposed to do it. We mustn't neglect our duties.

"And above all, we must learn to endure. Even if it means falling down a hundred times, we must continue to get up, and do battle. Life is about failures and learning to overcome them. We must develop an iron will. Don't be a quitter. We have to face our faults at some point in time. They're not going to fall away on their own.

"Our tests and problems are a result of our past actions. God would be very unjust if he gave one person wealth and another person poverty or one person a healthy body and the other person a sickly one. We create these conditions ourselves. God is not a tyrant."

Adam followed Harish's advice completely. He meditated twice daily, once in the morning after rising and again in the evening before retiring. He practiced an affirmation given him by his friend. During his meditation and during the day, as often as he when he remembered, he affirmed over and over that he was a magnet of success.

Thoughts of Taneka were ever present in the back of Adam's mind. He wanted her companionship and needed her love. He tried seeing her as a mother. A mother's principal trait is love. Harish had reminded him that each person has two aspects of God, reason and emotion. In man, reason is predominant, in women, emotion. Every person needs to strive for a perfect balance of the two. Once balanced, we free ourselves forever of the limited ego and the confinements of the world.

Adam's practices began paying off. He soon was seeing both the world and himself differently. He became more aware of his hidden desires and negative opinions. Harish told him to be careful of negativity. We must not judge others. By judging others we attract that trait to ourselves. Often what we see is something that we have within ourselves. When we pass judgment on another person we're actually passing judgment on ourselves. Additionally, by passing judgments, we end up hiding from our own faults. However, it's all right to character read, just don't judge. Character reading helps prevent us from falling into the wrong company.

Harish also told him it's good to learn from another's mistakes. That way we don't have to go through them ourselves.

The following day Harish arrived at Adam's home; four books were under his arm. "Are you ready for more lessons?" He asked.

"Inside or outside today?"

"The weather's too nice to stay in. Let's go out again on your patio."

"What's with those four books you're carrying?"

"They're for you," Harish said. "Here, take them."

Each book was a biography. They were the lives of Padre Pio, Saint Francis of Assisi, Ramakrishna, and Ammachi.

"Adam, have you finished reading Yogananda's autobiography?"

"Yes, it was fascinating but I'm still questioning its validity."

"I'm loaning you these books today in hopes that they'll help you understand the nature of our world. Truth is often stranger than fiction."

"What's so special about these four people?"

"Padre Pio was a Catholic priest and Saint Francis a Catholic monk. Both were Italian and both took on the stigmata of Christ."

"Christ's wounds," Adam responded.

"That's right. Padre Pio lived in the twentieth century. He was broad-minded and tolerant of all true religions. He had several spiritual experiences as did Saint Francis, to whom Jesus appeared nightly. Another interesting fact about Padre Pio and Saint Francis is that they both had healing abilities.

"Ramakrishna was a great soul and considered a fully realized Master or Satguru. He lived in India in the nineteenth century. He taught that there's only one God, who is omnipresent. There is only one religion, the religion of God. There is only one language, the language of the Heart, and that there is only one caste, the caste of humanity.

"Ammachi is known as the 'The Hugging Saint.' She also is from India and currently travels to this country once or twice a year to give darshan to those wishing to see her. Darshan is the receiving of a spiritual blessing from one who is self-realized, one who actually knows God. Ammachi teaches selfless service, the helping of others without any thought of personal gain."

"I've heard of her," Adam admitted. "Edwina gave Taneka some reading material about her."

"These books should broaden your awareness and validate many points brought up in Yogananda's work. He started an organization called Self-Realization Fellowship. But you already know that."

"Yes, that's right. Taneka and I loved the SRF Gardens in Encinitas."

"It's a beautiful place and so peaceful," Harish stated. "Any way, SRF, the short name for it, is a nonprofit organization. Yogananda formulated a three year series of weekly lessons. They provide a detailed study of both learning and living the spiritual life. Anyone interested in these lessons may apply for them. Yogananda was a Satguru, one with God. His role was to show the essential unity between the teachings of Christ and Krishna."

"Yes, that's mentioned in his book."

"The words Christ and Krishna are similar in spelling, and both have the same meaning. Krishna is considered the Christ of India. Krishna is my Satguru, Edwina's is Christ. Adam, you need to find yours. When one is ready God sends a fully-realized Master. The bond is eternal. The Master is responsible for the liberation of his devotee, even if this means lifetimes. Eventually, under the Master's guidance, the devotee experiences and knows God.

"Are there Masters living in physical bodies now?" Adam asked.

"Yes. Mahavatar Babaji, Ammachi and Mother Meera come to mind at the moment. A Master doesn't have to be in a physical body in order to help his devotee. Look at how many devotees Jesus Christ has."

"Millions," Adam answered.

"As do Buddha, Krishna, Mohammed, and a host of others."

"I see," Adam claimed. "How did the Masters come to be?"

"Once they were like you and I. Through years of inner work they became self-realized. Self-realization is knowing through the depths of your soul that you are one with the omnipresence of God. Jesus told us we are all sons of God and know not."

"And we all can do the work needed to reach self-realization?"

"Adam, we must do it. In fact, eventually we'll have to do it. God will see to it. We must know who we are. Once we find our way back to perfection we'll also find perfect love. God is this."

"We are all perfect sons of God," Adam said with conviction.

"That's right, Adam. We are like jets in a gas burner. There are many little holes through which the ignited gas is pouring, but under the burner is but one flame. We are the little flames coming from the big flame of Life."

"That's a beautiful way of looking at it," Adam conveyed.

Harish went on to explain the nature of teachers. He said that on the spiritual path one may have many teachers but only one Satguru. The disciple must give his Master complete loyalty. People make the mistake of blindly following those who don't know God. These leaders may know the scriptures but they don't know the inner meanings of the scriptures.

Most religions are not doing their jobs, Harish claimed. They should be leading people to the actual experience of God. It isn't enough to go to church one day a week, hear a brief sermon, then return home and go back to the old way of life. Where's the spiritual progress in this? He asked. He then pointed out that religion needs to show mankind how to do the inner work. We mustn't be 'Sunday Christians.' It isn't enough to worship Jesus because he is Jesus.

Christians must embrace the universal ideals he taught and strive to be like him. They need to seek out the deeper meanings of his teachings. Jesus was crucified once but his teachings are crucified daily due to the misinterpretations of his words by limited minds.

"God created His Lila, His Divine Play, for both His and our enjoyment. Life is simple, we've made it complex. We've fallen into the hands of delusion. That is the 'Fall of Man.' He gave us free will and we misused it. God is not a dictator. He would never force His will on us or take away our free will. In His loving patience He waits for us to turn to Him. He is the source of all peace, happiness, and love."

"But why does God permit evil in His play?" Adam asked.

"Evil provides a contrast that enables us to know and experience goodness. Evil is the test of God to see if we will choose Him or His toys. Remember, we have free will to do either."

Adam finally received the news he had been waiting for. Taneka was going to spend a day with him. They were going on an afternoon outing in the Superstition Mountains. Harish and Edwina would be joining them.

The night before the outing Harish gave Adam the last of his lessons. Harish discussed the nature of material possessions. He told Adam that every time we waste power going after unnecessary material possessions we are further away from the magnetism that attracts God. Adam found this to be an interesting concept. Looking at it this way, man has a certain amount of energy at his disposal and that energy is a force that can be used to attract whatever is wanted.

He told this to Harish who agreed with him but warned about wants and desires. He added that what's attracted, good or bad, will eventually come, be it days, months or years. He also said that a person whose concentration is scattered in material ambitions only continues to feel a restless lack of fulfillment in his soul. Material possessions alone cannot make life secure. Happiness cannot be found in a disorganized life that doesn't balance material pursuits with spirituality. It's simply foolish to spend one's life seeking things that must be forsaken at the time of death.

The day of the outing arrived! Adam and Taneka were together at last! The two of them were on the hiking trail within the Superstition Mountains. Harish and Edwina had gone on ahead of the reunited pair.

Adam and Taneka parked themselves on a large flat rock in a dry creek bed. Behind them and to their right in the distance the Superstition mountain range projected up from the desert floor into a blue sky. In a few days it would officially be spring. Yet it already felt like spring to Adam. He was renewed, invigorated. His life was once again on the rise. Without Taneka his existence had become dormant. He might just have well have spent the winter months sleeping in a cave. But, then again, if that had happened, he wouldn't be where he is now. He would not have made the effort needed to bring Taneka back to him and there wouldn't have been any personal growth.

"You don't know how happy I feel being with you today," Adam said.

"I think I know," Taneka claimed.

"I want to spend the rest of my life with you," he said taking her hand in his.

She pulled her hand away from his. "I'm here as your friend," she said.

"I want you as a friend and lover," he retorted.

Taneka made no reply so Adam took out a water bottle from his back and handed it to her. She put it to her lips, drank some, then set the bottle down on her free side.

"I've been working hard trying to overcome my imperfections," he said hoping to convince her that he had changed.

"Your sister has been giving me progress reports."

"Did I get any A's?"

Taneka laughed. "Some," she said.

"Then you see some good in me."

"There has always been good in you, Adam."

"And the rest of me?" He asked wanting her forgiveness for everything.

"The rest of you is a question mark."

"Are you willing to work with the question mark?"

"Yes," she said.

He leaned over to kiss her. She moved away.

"Can't we be lovers?"

"At this point we are friends only."

"Then I want to be your best friend," he claimed.

"I'm opening my heart to you now as a best friend. I want only what's best for you," she told him.

"You are what's best for me, Tan. I want us to perfect our love. I'll patiently wait for the time when we become both friends and lovers."

"You must learn to live above the physical plain, Adam."

"I'm going to make my love pure and unselfish so that it reflects divine love."

"I'll be looking for evidence of your pureness and unselfishness."

"You'll have it, Tan."

"If we're going to make this work, we must create an atmosphere of tolerance, forgiveness and trust in one another."

"Believe me, we'll create that atmosphere. It will be the water that feeds the plant of our love."

"I do rather miss our romance," Taneka admitted.

"As do I," Adam agreed.

"We better go and meet up with Harish and Edwina. They're waiting for us."

They once more made their way on the trail beside the creek bed. They hiked about ten minutes then came to a narrow canyon on their left. They went through it and in a short while they found their friends resting by a pond.

"You've found the springs," Edwina shouted when they came into view. "Harish and I were about to have lunch, now we all can eat together."

"You both look happy," Harish told them.

"We've reached an agreement," Adam said.

"Good, then come and sit down next to us," Edwina requested.

The four friends began eating the sandwiches and chips that they had carried in their packs. Taneka asked Harish and Edwina about their recent travels. Edwina fondly expressed the wonderful feelings she had had at the sacred sites visited. She said the Himalayas were awesome in their beauty. They had made a trek to the source of the Ganges River. She understood why the Indian people held it in such high regard.

"You know," Edwina went on, "the Himalayan landscape was fresh, as if God's hand had just come down, sculptured and painted everything."

"How wonderful," Taneka exclaimed.

"Yes, it truly was," Edwina agreed. "And being with those holy men and women brought me to another level of awareness."

"Harish, what do you think?" Taneka asked him.

"Spiritual energy is like that. It's uplifting. Once you taste it you want more."

"Someday I hope to taste that energy," Adam wished out loud.

"The germ of success in whatever you want to accomplish is in your willpower, Adam. Once your course it set and your will is firm you are on your way to success."

"Is this how you see success, Harish? If one sets his mind, persists, and uses his willpower success will be his," Taneka asked him.

"Absolutely! Success needs a determined will. There mustn't be physical or mental laziness. We must never give up. We should say to ourselves each day that this day may be the very day I will succeed."

"And if it isn't?" Adam asked.

"Then we just do our best that day and forget about the next one. We never want to burden the soul with petty worries. We just accept what comes and know we've done our best. Tomorrow is another day."

"How about we all go in one of these ponds by us," Edwina wished out loud.

"That would be refreshing," Adam conveyed.

"I'm game," Taneka said.

"What kind?' Adam asked her.

"A deer," she said.

"Two legged or four legged?" He responded.

"Four today, Adam.

"That's too bad, I'd prefer you to be the two legged variety."

"Tomorrow's another day," Taneka claimed.

"Then I'll patiently wait for the next dawn," Adam concluded.

At mid-afternoon the two couples left the springs and began hiking back to the car. They reached an area thick with bushes and treaded carefully through it. Snakes and other desert creatures were out of hibernation and the foliage offered them an escape from the hot sun. The four hikers made it through the brush safely, the path opened up into a wide, dry river bed allowing them to walk alongside one another. Talking became easier, they were contented, and within this contentment they began speaking of happiness and how it can be found.

Edwina said everyone must differentiate between their needs and wants. She pointed out that the more one depends upon conditions outside oneself for happiness the less happiness one experiences. Everyone agreed with that. Harish added that happiness can be secured by self-control and nurturing plain living, high thinking, and by spending less money. Adam felt control of emotions was extremely important and that one must possess courage, faith and hope in order to feel real happiness. Harish made the comment that one mustn't neglect duty because it is actually action that must be taken care of. If we don't fulfill our duties we cannot be happy with ourselves. The conversation was concluded by everyone agreeing that nonattachment to all things and keeping mainly to true necessities are ways to happiness and these will take away restlessness and lead one to contentment.

"That went by fast, here we are already back at the car," Edwina told everyone as they approached the vehicle.

"Time goes by when you're having fun," Taneka spoke out.

"It's good to have all of us back together," Adam commented. "I don't know what I'd do without my good friends," he added.

"Friendship is a thing to be treasured. It's another gift from our Creator," Harish imparted.

"I'm grateful we're all here now," Adam told them. "I've been going through a long, rough, and ragged period."

"And what about me, Adam? How do you think the past has affected me?" Taneka asked him.

Adam looked at the others and then to Taneka. "I think I can truthfully say that I know what you've experienced. And for that I am truly sorry. Believe me, I'm not the same person I was before all of this began."

"I'm beginning to believe you. You know I've had to change too," Taneka made known.

"Then we've both changed. I wonder if we've experienced these same problems in our past lives together,' Adam mused out loud.

"We must have in some way or we wouldn't still be facing them," Taneka answered.

"We're here to help one another get off the wheel, the wheel that's keeping us on this mud ball called Earth," Adam declared decisively.

"You're right," Harish told them. "We've been like caged hamsters spinning round and round on its enclosed wheel," Harish added and then laughed out loud.

Chapter 12

Spring

To love is to release God's unlimited storehouse of golden treasure.

Spring is a time of renewal, rebirth, and resurrection. Nature shows us this and asks, "Death where is thy sting?"

The seed of Adam and Taneka's love was growing in the soil of their hearts. It had been there all the time just needing the water of devotion for nourishment. And now, with spring's arrival, that seed of love would be given the opportunity to sprout into the beautiful flower it truly was.

Emails, phone calls, occasional lunches and dinners kept Adam and Taneka in touch daily. They became best friends. Their souls were being intertwined by the vines of love growing secretly around them.

Although not admitting it to herself, Taneka was ready to accept Adam fully back into her life. Their separation had been a time of reassessment, a time of inner work for both of them. If Adam was willing to change, then she must also change. She had to let go of her uncontrolled emotions and insecurities as well as work unselfishly with Adam.

Taneka knew without a shadow of a doubt that Adam was her soulmate. Soulmates come together to grow together. They take the seed of their physical love and water it with devotion until it blossoms into divine love. Their partnership must be a willing sharing of the others difficulties. And ever before them must lie the goal of eternal oneness and the joy that is in that oneness.

Dinner together at fine restaurants, soft lights, moonlight cruises, these thoughts filled Edwina with waves of tenderness as she sat across from Adam on his patio.

"I'd say I'm falling in love all over again with you, Adam. But, then again, I've never been out of love with you."

"There's never been a time when I've not loved you also," Adam let her know.

"I wish it didn't have to be so difficult. Men want their toys, human or otherwise. Women want their securities. I'm proud of you, Adam. The effort you're making to change yourself pleases me greatly."

"I sold my Cobra to Ray."

"Oh, why did you do that?"

"It was an unnecessary necessity."

Taneka pondered over his answer then asked, "What about the sexual problem?"

"I'm still celibate."

"Good, keep it up."

"If I do that you'll have to be a good runner."

Taneka smiled. "Then I'd better buy myself a pair of track shoes."

It was mid-April in the Valley of the Sun. Stewart had arranged for a picnic along the shores of the Salt River. Taneka, Harish and Edwina had mixed feelings about the outing. Adam convinced them to go. He said there weren't many sub-one hundred degree days left. By the time May arrived the intensity of the desert's heat would increase and force them inside or up into the high mountains.

Adam rose early, ate a quick breakfast, and then began tidying up his house. He cleaned for a half hour. There still was twenty minutes left before his friends were due for arrival. He went into the study, picked up Ramakrishna's biography from his desk and sat down on the desk's chair. Opening the book at random his eyes fell on a curious passage; it was an analogy about doing the inner work. Adam read, 'Life is like a swiftly flowing river. When you seek God, you swim against the current of worldly tendencies that pull your mind toward limited material and sensory consciousness. You must make the effort to swim 'upstream' every moment. If you relax, the strong current of delusion will carry you away. Your efforts must be constant.'

Boy did he get that right, Adam thought. Trying to find peace after it's fallen into the current of restlessness and desires is like swimming upstream against a powerful current. The illusory world wants to carry you one way and you want to go the other way.

Adam read a while longer, closed the book, and then set it back on his desk. He stood up, left the room and made his way into the garage. He came back into the house carrying an ice chest. He went into the kitchen and filled the chest with food and beverages. Shortly thereafter his three friends arrived. Adam, with Harish's help, gathered everything that was needed for the picnic and together they packed it into Adam's Tahoe. Soon the four of them were on their way to the river outing.

They drove for nearly forty minutes. Approaching the Salt Riverr Adam pulled into a small area off the road. Five cars were there, he found an open spot between two of them and parked within it. It was close to noon. The rest of the party would soon be arriving from their float trip. They had arrived earlier, left their cars, and then driven several miles further up the main road in a passenger van. The van pulled a trailer loaded with three rafts. Their destination was a launching point for the float down the river.

It was going to be a hot day; the temperature had already reached the nineties. Adam and Harish unloaded the car and carried everything to a clearing next to scattered bushes and trees. They set up four folding chairs, sat amongst the shade visiting, and waited. A half hour passed this way and then three rafts came around the river's bend floating towards them.

"It's Stewart and the others," Adam announced.

In the lead raft were Stewart and Ashley, behind it a larger one carrying Richard, Desiree, Sam, Jaya, Ray, and Vicki. Bringing up the rear in a smaller raft were Dinar and Melia.

Stewart steered towards the shore. When he was near enough to be heard he shouted out, "It's a great trip, too bad you didn't join us! The float down the river was effortless!"

Adam and Harish walked over to the river bank. They helped secure the rafts to the shore and then waited for everyone to step ashore. Once everyone was together on land items were brought out from the nearby cars and the picnic area was set up. Two barbecues, three folding tables, chairs and ice chests were laid out in the flat area next to the trees and bushes.

"I didn't know you two would be here," Harish said to Dinar and Melia.

"It was Stewart's wish," Dinar told his cousin. "And what about you?"

"Adam convinced me to come today."

"I'm glad you did," Dinar said.

"How's your expanded business doing?"

"We're making good progress. Stewart anticipates another expansion next year."

"Won't that put you under greater financial stress?"

"Stewart told me not to worry about it. He'll make things work."

"You'll be putting yourself more into his hands," Harish claimed.

"Dinar and Stewart are both good business men. They'll make it work," Melia said joining the conversation.

"And how do you fit into all of this?" Harish asked her.

"I'm now managing a Far East Imports store," she said proudly.

"I hope you do well. Just don't get in over you heads with Demaya," Harish warned them.

"Don't worry about us, cousin, we know what we're doing," Dinar claimed.

"There you are!" Adam called out walking over and joining them.

"Tan and I are going in for a swim. Would anyone like to join us?"

"Melia and I are going to help prepare the food for our meal," Dinar answered.

"I'll go in the river with you," Harish said. He and Adam went over to their picnic site. Edwina and Taneka were waiting for them there.

"Edwina, we're going in for a swim, how about you?" Harish asked her.

"It's getting pretty hot. A refreshing dip sounds good to me."

The two couples made their way to the water. Desiree was near them at the river's edge staring out at the water. She turned and looked in their direction.

"Hi, Adam," she said and then faced Taneka. "I didn't know you two were back together."

"We are," Taneka replied. "Adam's just too irresistible."

Desiree grinned. "I know," she said and then walked smugly away.

"Come on, Adam, let's go in that water now," Taneka requested.

Adam took her hand and led her into the river. Harish and Edwina joined them.

"That Desiree can be a real bitch," Edwina declared.

"You're right," Taneka let out.

"Let's swim to the other side, Edwina," Harish said. "We'll see you both over there," he told his friends and then he and Edwina swam on to the opposite shore.

Adam and Taneka waded further out; the water was now up to their chests. A stick floated down the river and went between them making the water appear divided. After it moved on and the water between them was once again one they embraced one another and then submerged themselves in the water. When they came back up they were clean. The sum total of their feelings for one another had concentrated within their hearts, it was pure and they were pure, it was joy and they were joy, this was now the totality of their existence.

"Tan, I have something for you," Adam told her. "I can't give it to you here. We need to swim over to the other side of the river where Harish and Edwina are now. The current is strong and we'll have to swim a bit upstream in order to cross over to them."

They set out, their feet left the river's bottom, they swam to the middle of the river, and struggled within the strength of the current. With greater effort Adam and Taneka increased their strokes and finally made it to the safely of the other side.

"It took some exertion on you part but you're here now," Harish told them after they were settled.

"I watched you two embrace before you left," Edwina let them know. "Does that mean you're an item once again?"

Adam smiled. He opened a hidden pocket in his swimsuit, reached in, and came out with a zip-locked plastic bag that contained a small, blue velvet box.

"What do you have there, Brother?" Edwina wanted to know.

Adam removed the box from the plastic bag. He opened it and revealed Taneka's engagement ring.

"Taneka, please accept this ring from me," he said then took out the ring and placed it in the palm of her right hand.

"Look at it closely, Tan."

She raised her palm to eye level. "What am I supposed to see?"

"Look inside the ring."

She did as he asked. "There's something inscribed in it."

"Go ahead, read it," he requested.

"It says, 'In God all things are possible.' How sweet, Adam."

Adam dropped to one knee. "Will you marry me, Tan?"

Her eyes filled with tears. "Yes," she answered.

He stood up and placed the ring on her finger. They embraced and kissed.

"Congratulations," Edwina yelled out. "This time you will be my sister-in-law," she said joyfully.

"She will,' Harish affirmed.

The four of them sat down together along the bank of the river, pleased with the way things were turning out. They began talking about the past year, how it had been a time of change, trials, and spiritual growth. Each knew they had a path to follow, each one having to walk their own walk wearing the shoes of their inner work. Psychological kinks and imperfections were the pebbles, rocks and boulders on the path leading to their journey's end.

"We better go back now," Harish said. "The picnic is in full swing and we still have things to do."

The two couples swam back through the current and on to the other side of the river. Sitting by the trees were Stewart and his crew watching and waiting like vultures for the time to catch and hold their prey in their hungry jaws.

"Good, we're all here. It's time to picnic," Demaya claimed with their arrival.

A full array of food was set out on two tables. A line was formed and then each one present selected his nourishment and went on to sit in a chair to enjoy it.

Richard sat between Desiree and Ashley. "I'm ready for a feast," he claimed.

Desiree spoke out to Adam and Taneka who were sitting nearby. "I've been waiting for you," she told them. Before they could reply something caught her attention and she turned away from Adam and Taneka.

Richard was caressing Ashley's hips. Desiree's eyes filled with venom. Abruptly, she got up from here chair and went over to Adam. "I was watching you and Taneka when you were on the other side of the river," she told him.

"Then you saw Adam give me this ring," Taneka said holding her hand up to her. "We're engaged."

"You'll be happy, Taneka, Adam's a great bed partner!" She announced loudly so that all could hear.

"Haven't you done enough damage already!" Taneka shouted back at her.

Desiree's face burned. She glared at Taneka with her green, venomous eyes, reached out and pushed her into the bushes. A coiled snake, unseen by all, hissed then lunged out and bit into Taneka. Adam stood up, seized his chair, swung it wildly at the serpent and drove it off. Then he turned to Desiree.

"You're an evil woman!" He shouted at her. "Go crawl back into the hole you belong in!"

Harish grabbed ahold of Desiree and dragged here over to Richard. "Take this woman!" He ordered.

Richard was too stunned by the chain of events and did not move. Ashley, however, stood up and went over to Stewart who was casually observing the scene being played out before him.

"Taneka can't tolerate poison," Adam yelled out. "Harish get my keys from our table," he asked him urgently then bent down, picked Taneka up in his arms and made his way to his car.

Harish went to their table, grabbed the car keys from it, and then went over to Stewart. "You're behind all of this," he yelled at him.

Demaya glared back at Harish. "What do you know?" He said calmly.

"I know there's more to you than you let on," Harish responded.

Demaya laughed at him. "You're delusionary," he told him.

"You would like the others to believe that, wouldn't you, Demaya? But we both know the opposite is true," Harish answered and then hurried to Adam's car.

Harish opened the back seat's passenger's door. Adam placed Taneka on the seat and got in next to her. Harish and Edwina hopped in the front seats and then they drove off.

"We'll go to the hospital in Scottsdale, it's the closest," Harish informed them.

"Taneka, talk to me, you have to stay with me," Adam commanded.

Taneka tried to speak but was unable to; she was slipping into unconsciousness. Adam shook her. She opened her eyes and gave

Adam a most loving look. "I will be yours always, Adam," she said with a conviction that came from her soul. Then there was nothing.

"What's happening back there?" Edwina asked.

"She's been going in and out of consciousness."

"You have to keep her awake," Harish told him.

Adam kept shaking her. Her eyes opened partially. "Stay with me, Tan, stay with me," he said again and again.

It seemed like an eternity. Finally they reached the hospital. The staff at the ER realizing the seriousness of Taneka's condition rushed her into a room. Adam went with her, Harish and Edwina stayed in the waiting area. A doctor arrived on the scene. Adam told him about Taneka's intolerance to venom and that her mother had died from it.

"We have to prevent her from going into a coma," the doctor informed him, "and we have to stop the poison from reaching her heart and other vital organs," he added. He then gave her a shot which was an antidote for the poison that was in her system. "If she doesn't come around soon she'll have to be taken upstairs," the doctor made clear.

Time moved ever so slowly. Adam went out to the waiting area and told Harish and his sister what was happening. They tried consoling him. His shock was too deep and their words went over his head. He left them and returned to Taneka.

"We're taking her upstairs," the doctor told him as he entered the room.

After rushing Taneka to the hospital a major tiff occurred at the river. Richard wanted to know why Desiree had been so mean and pushed Taneka into the bushes and the snake. They argued, and in the course of the argument the truth came out about each other's affair.

"You didn't have to seduce Adam!" Richard yelled at her.

"Yeah, and you didn't have to screw Ashley either, did you!" She screamed back at him.

"We both have our sex lives, you know that!" He shouted out.

At this point Vicki came over and joined in the argument. "Hey, it's just sex you two, you should be well aware of that by now. You've still got each other."

"That's right, Desiree, we've got each other," Richard repeated.

Desiree stared at him with dangerous, dagger-like eyes. "I want to leave now," she ordered. "Take me home."

Stewart Demaya and the others remained in the background watching the scene. Ashley was by Stewart's side. He whispered something into her ear and she nodded back at him. The others simply stood by observing what was happening.

Richard and Desiree left still arguing with each other. They went on into his car and raced off down the road.

Dinar spoke to Melia standing next to him. "I wonder what's going to happen next."

"I don't know," she said, "but I'm sure everything will turn out just the way it's supposed to."

Adam nervously walked along beside the bed as the nurse wheeled Taneka along the corridors and into the elevator. They went up two floors. Taneka was taken to a room directly across from the nurse's station. Two nurses came into the room and immediately placed monitors on Taneka.

A new doctor entered the room. He immediately went over to Taneka and checked her vital signs. When he was finished he turned to Adam.

"I'm Doctor Goodwin," he told him.

Adam introduced himself.

"We will give your fiancé the best of help, Adam. Unfortunately it's going to be a waiting game. Rest assured we'll be keeping an eye on her. The nurses are close by and they will monitor her constantly."

"Thank you, doctor."

"I'll be back as needed," Doctor Goodwin said and then left the room.

Adam moved a chair next to Taneka's bed. He put his hand on hers. "Taneka, you stay with me," he said speaking into her ear. "We're going to get married and we're going to spiritualize our marriage. Our love will be one love, and it will grow, grow into divine love. You have my word on that."

"Any changes?"

Adam turned around. Harish and Edwina were behind him. "Doctor Goodwin says it's going to be a waiting game."

"Then we'll be here waiting with you," Edwina told him.

Harish placed two chairs along the wall across from Taneka's bed and then he and Edwina sat down there.

"What do you do in a time like this?" Adam asked him.

"Pray," Harish answered.

"How?"

"Pray to God with all your heart, Adam. Have faith in Him. Remember He sees things by the whole, and we see them in parts. Whatever happens, in the end, it is what's best for us."

"I wish I knew who my spiritual Master is," Adam spoke out loud.

"The Master will come when you're ready," Harish assured him.

Edwina spoke out. "I've been praying to Jesus, Adam. Harish has been praying to Krishna. It doesn't matter how we pray, as long as we're sending our prayers to God, or through a Master who's one with Him."

One of the monitoring machines next to Taneka went off. A nurse immediately came into the room and checked to see what was happening. She pushed a nearby button. After a few moments Doctor Goodwin arrived, went to Taneka and examined her. Then he spoke to Adam.

"I'm afraid she's slipped into a coma. There's nothing else we can do for her at this time." Doctor Goodwin patted Adam on his shoulder then left the room.

"Oh, God," Adam said. Tears were rolling down his face. "Don't you do this, Tan, come back to me, come back to me."

Hours went by. Nurses came in and out of the room at regular intervals. Harish and Edwina remained with Adam. They occupied the time by recalling fond memories, the enjoyable times the four of them had had together, the climb up Mount Humphries, the trip to Reno, the desert hikes, the dinners, movies and their spiritual discussions.

Adam's emotions began to settle somewhat. "Edwina, tell me about your recent travel," he asked her.

288

"Adam," she began, "we had any unusual experience when we were in the Himalayas. We met a holy man there. I'll let Harish finish the story."

"The saint told us he had met a man who had an unselfish devotion to his wife. He deeply loved her. After she died he wandered for years seeking a way to find her. That's how he came to be in the Himalayas. When the man came to him, the saint was unaware of this. The man convinced the saint to give spiritual initiation to both he and his wife. The saint agreed and asked him where she was. That's when the man told him she had passed away. The saint had given his word so he told the man to sit in meditation. The holy man then proceeded to invoke the presence of the wife. She appeared suddenly. She and her husband talked for a long time and then the saint initiated and blessed them. The wife soon departed. It was then that the man realized the beloved form of his wife was in reality an individualized manifestation of God and that this was an example of divine love. Due to the man's unselfish love for his wife, that love was transmuted into divine love."

"That's an incredible story," Adam exclaimed. "In God all things are possible."

"Yes, they are, Adam. Don't ever give up hope."

It was now after midnight; Taneka's condition remained unchanged. Adam touched her face. "She should be refreshed. I'm going to wash her face and hands," he announced, then stood up and went on into the bathroom.

He did not immediately return. Edwina went to check on him. Adam was standing over the sink washing his own face.

"What are doing, Adam, I thought you were going to wash Taneka?"

"Oh, my gosh," he said, "I thought I was washing her."

They returned to the room. Adam went over to Taneka and washed her with the cleansing cloth he had brought with him. When he was done he gave the cloth to Edwina and then sat down next to Taneka. He put her hand into his.

"Tan, I know you can hear me. I want you to know that I've found in you all that I have sought in the forest of time. I see in your face all the dreams of my fulfilled desires. Listen to me, you shall come out of this coma and when you do we shall fly from star to star whether it be from this side of eternity or its other side."

The night hours moved towards sunrise.

"Adam, Doctor Goodwin is here," Edwina said breaking the silence around them.

"Let's see how your girl is doing," the doctor said to them. He checked the monitors. His face grew serious. He placed a stethoscope on Taneka's chest. "I was afraid of this. Her breathing has become shallower," he told them.

"What's that mean?" Adam asked him.

"I'm sorry, Adam," he said solemnly. "Her body is starting to shut down. I'm afraid it's just a matter of time now."

"Matter of time, everything's just a matter of time," Adam said angrily.

The doctor peered over at Edwina and Harish, looked at Adam and then shook his head. "I'm sorry," he said once more.

Edwina went to Adam and put her arm around him. He squeezed his sister's hand with his free one. "She can't go, Edwina. We have so much yet to experience, so much to accomplish. If I have to, I will bring her back down through the heavens to me."

Edwina placed her arm around his neck and hugged him tightly. He glanced up at her through his watery eyes and saw her love.

Adam moved Taneka's hand closer to him. 'Tan," he spoke softly, "come back to me. Our love is the thread that holds the beads of our hearts together. Come back to me. I'm pulling you back by the thread that binds us. I'm pulling you back to me now."

Adam thought he felt a movement in her hand. "She's coming back now," he announced to the others.

Harish went over to Edwina and Adam. He bent over and put his ear to Taneka's mouth. He stayed that way for a few seconds then straightened up. "Adam, she's barely breathing. Her breaths are so shallow."

"That cannot be," Adam said, and then once more, put his mouth to Taneka's ear. "Come back to me, Tan, come back to me, Tan."

He waited for a response. There was none. He became despondent. He heard an inner voice telling him it was useless. The voice told him Taneka was better off on the other side. Just let her go. Don't stay now, there's nothing you can do.

Doubts came to Adam and his faith left him. The voice told him to leave now, don't watch her slip away. You don't need to see this.

"I won't just sit here and watch her die!" Adam shouted out loudly He stood up angrily, leaned over and kissed Taneka and then stomped out of the room.

"Harish do something," Edwina pleaded.

He shook his head twice. "Adam needs his space. He has something to work out. When it's done he'll return."

"How do you know this?" She asked him.

He smiled wisely at her. "Edwina, trust me. Adam's inner strength will bring him back to us."

Adam raced down the hallway to the stairway and then skipped down them and out of the hospital. It was dawn. The sky was ominous, dark and depressing. He hopped into his car, tossed his cell phone on the seat next to him and roared off. He drove on aimlessly for a while and then he felt a sudden urge to turn right at the next street. He passed a school and scanned its playground. The children weren't out yet for their lessons. He pulled his car off to the side of the rode and looked over at the school grounds. He felt that something was waiting there for him. As he stared there a dark figure came into view.

Adam drove to the school's lot and parked there. He grabbed his cell phone then stepped out of the car. His mind was full of anguish and held 'what ifs.' The past is the past Harish had told him. You can't change that. You can only live in the now. Adam's now was pain. He had regained his soulmate only to lose her once more. What would he do without her? If only he hadn't been weak and had controlled his desires. If only he had used his will and had done what was right. If only he wasn't attached to his possessions. The sun was in its sixth hour. Adam closed the car door, stuffed the cell phone in his pocket, and then walked to the figure which was now standing in the playground.

"Ah, you have come, my friend. You have made the right decision," the man told him as Adam approached him.

"Stewart!" Adam called out surprised. "What are you doing here?"

"You have lost your girl. I am here to help you move past this," Demaya claimed.

"I've just lost my soulmate, how can you help that?" Adam said gloomily.

"There are no soulmates, Adam. Harish has filled your head with falsehoods."

"What does Harish have to do with all of this?" Adam asked him.

"He has been leading you the wrong way," Demaya told him.

"You're wrong; he's been helping me with my problems."

"Your problems are overblown, Adam. You have started looking in the wrong places for happiness and have turned away from what I have to offer. The world is yours for the taking. Everything you need and want is here for you. Anything you think you have lost is easily replaced with something greater." Demaya told him all this as if he were the master holding the key to happiness.

Adam thought briefly about Stewart's words. Then Taneka came into his mind and he let it dwell there. He turned fully inward and touched what was the—the sprouted seed of their love. Its strength rose within him. "Stewart," he spoke out with a voice full of conviction, "True love has no need of replacement. True love is never lost and always remains a part of the soul."

"Again you use the words of Harish," Demaya spoke, this time his voice shaking with anger. "Follow my ways, Adam. You'll have even more satisfying women than Desiree," he added.

The mention of Desiree's name threw Adam into a sea of emotion. Once again he felt weakness. Demaya immediately seized the opportunity of snaring what he wanted.

"You know your desires, Adam. I am here to fulfill them. Tell me what you want and as I speak they shall be yours," Demaya claimed deceitfully.

"You have such powers?"

"I do," Demaya said.

Adam's cell phone rang interrupting them. He removed it from his pocket and answered the call. It was Edwina.

"Hello," he said expecting to hear the worse.

"Adam, it's a miracle. Taneka has come out of her coma. She's asking for you."

"What!" He answered, not fully believing his ears.

"I said Taneka's waiting anxiously to see you."

"I'll be there as quickly as I can," he told his sister and then closed up the phone.

Stewart heard their words. "Don't go. There's nothing there for you," he said impatiently.

Adam faced him squarely. "Who are you really, Stewart?"

"What do you mean?"

"You have been behind everything," Adam said decisively. His emotions were settling down; reasoning was returning.

"Behind what?" Demaya asked knowing that he had underestimated Adam.

"I realize now that it's been you putting thoughts of doubt, desire , and despair into my mind."

"How could I do that? Your desires and weaknesses are yours alone." His face was now dark and twisted.

"I know who you are, you're an agent of evil," Adam exclaimed.

Demaya laughed wickedly. "I'm not evil, the evil is within you."

"No, you create and play with it. You need souls and capture them in your net of delusion."

Demaya cackled. "It's not I creating evil, Adam. It's He who you call God. Go look in Isaiah 45:6,7. You'll find the words, "I am the Lord and there is none else. I form the light, and create darkness: I make peace, and create evil: I the Lord do all these things."

"Why are you telling me this? Are you making excuses for you ways?"

"Go ask the one you call God, it's His play. The world you see before you was given to me to care for. It's as simple as that. He uses me and I use you," Demaya revealed to Adam knowing now that his grip on him was slipping away.

"God, then, has his reasons. And you, you're doing a lousy job here," Adam claimed. "There's so much misery and waste. Why do you crave human souls?

"Men's souls give me my existence and my hold on this world. Without man's ego and its petty desires and habits my rule would end. But that shan't be the case. You and your kind have fallen hopelessly under the spell of delusion. You won't get off the wheel that holds you here."

"You are the one that fell; you are the one that chose to be evil!"

"What's the matter, Adam, don't you like my allies! Don't you like desire, doubt, delusion, denial, despair, and devastation?" Demaya hissed at him wickedly.

"My soulmate is calling out for me; it's not Stewart Demaya that I turn to. The seeds of weakness that you planted in me have been shattered by the totality of divine love."

"You need me," Demaya said in one last attempt at keeping his prey.

"You're right, I do need you. You have shown me the difference between good and evil, right and wrong, love and hate."

"You and your love!" Demaya screeched loudly and with much anger. He knew now he had lost. darkness gathered around him, a sickening sticky mist, and then it was gone and he was gone.

Adam shook his head at what he had just experienced. He left the play field and went onto his car.

The sky was clear now and the sun's brightness covered the grounds and all that surrounded it. Adam opened the car door, sat down and breathed a sigh of relief. He practiced calming his mind and focusing on peace. Then, after readying himself, he started the car's engine and drove off. He was on his way to his soulmate, she who was helping him find true love. He began talking to Taneka mentally. He renewed his vow of loyalty. Then he talked to God. He told Him he would accept whatever was to be. He would no longer resist what came to him. Whatever would come he would face and learn its lesson. Then he made a simple prayer using his own words.

Adam pulled into the hospital's lot, parked there, and rushed into the hospital and on up to Taneka's room. Edwina and Harish greeted him. Taneka was sitting up in bed.

He went to her. Tears were streaming down the lovers' cheeks. He kissed her.

She spoke to him, her voice was weak. "Adam, I love you."

"I thought I'd lost you," he told her.

"Adam," she said with effort. "I was floating in the heavens. I saw a great light. It was so peaceful. I wanted to go into that light. Then I heard you calling for me. Your voice reached me from across the heavens. It was tugging and pulling me back to you."

"Adam, Edwina and I will leave you two to be alone," Harish said walking near them. "Oh, by the way, Dinar called me this morning. Richard and Desiree were in a horrible accident. After we left for the hospital yesterday they got into a terrible fight. They left the picnic grounds in his car. Apparently the argument raged on. Richard was driving fast and recklessly. He ended up rolling his car. He and Desiree were rushed to a hospital. Richard's legs were crushed. Desiree suffered broken bones and a facial laceration. She will recover from them. However, for the rest of her life, she'll be left with a noticeable facial scar. Richard most likely won't walk again."

"They're paying the price," Adam declared.

Harish agreed with him then he and Edwina left the room.

Adam placed Taneka's hand in his. "You're here with me," he whispered. "I've put everything aside for you."

"I've come back to be with you, Adam."

"Get well, Tan. We'll marry in June.

"I know," she replied.

The sweet fragrance of love filled their hearts. Everything stopped and there was only love. The past and future dissolved. Every atom, every cell of their bodies, their whole being opened to this love, Adam and Taneka were no longer two, but three—the lover, the beloved, and love itself.

Made in the USA
Charleston, SC
21 November 2013